FRONT-LINE HOSPITAL

THE STORY OF WESLEY GUILD HOSPITAL

ILESHA, NIGERIA

DR. C. ANDREW PEARSON,

OBE, MB.ChB, DTM, FMCGP(Nigeria), FWACP(GP)

To the Wesley Guilds, on their Centenary

ONE Heart, ONE Way, ONE Hundred

Copies of this book can be purchased direct from the author at a price of £5.50 each including post and packing:

Dr C A Pearson
2 Springfield Road
Bury St Edmunds
Suffolk IP33 3AN, UK
Fax: (0)1284 753890

Published by:
FSG Communications Ltd, Vine House, Fair Green, Reach, Cambridge CB5 OJD, UK.

ISBN 1 871188 04 0

Printed in Great Britain by Biddles Ltd, Hardwick Industrial Estate, King's Lynn, Norfolk PE30 4LS

CONTENTS

FOREWORD

DR. PAULINE M. WEBB, D.Theol, D.Litt, FKC

I find it hard to know how to describe this book and its profound effect upon me. I confess first to a personal interest in the Wesley Guild Hospital. I had heard stories of it from my earliest childhood. The very word 'Ilesha' was a magic sound to me, and I loved hearing my father's vivid accounts of the years when he was in Nigeria during the First World War and the hospital was little more than a dispensary and a dream of the future. From my youth I remember the thrill of great Wesley Guild rallies where there was always an impassioned appeal for the support of the growing medical work in Nigeria. But most vivid is the memory of my own visit to Ilesha. I still have the photograph of the baby I saw born in the maternity ward, wrapped in a brightly coloured blanket (knitted by Guilders) and held in the arms of a nurse wearing her hospital badge, an exact replica of the familiar Wesley Guild brooch. Above all, I shall never forget the fifth birthday party of Bodunde, the first little girl to be registered in the Child Research project at the village of Imesi–Ile, which was to save the lives of thousands of children under five and affect the pattern of child care throughout Nigeria and far beyond.

Hospital stories have a fascination all their own, as any script writer of a TV medical series knows well. This one is spell-binding in its own particular way. It is not so much a story of the patients at the Wesley Guild Hospital as of the place itself, and of the people who have served it through its years of both triumph and turmoil. It has been from the beginning a team gathered from all over the world. Among the many names of the personnel recorded in this book, there are vivid pen portraits of men and women whose commitment, allied with their professional skill, laid the foundations of a hospital still renowned for the quality of its caring and for the centrality of its faith. For example, there is the story of Sister Stella Liony, a black nurse from Britain who responded to a call heard in a Methodist service to go out to Africa to serve in the land of her forefathers. Having qualified as a nursing sister herself, she was able on arrival in Nigeria in 1922 to persuade many local girls to come for training and so began the nursing school at Ilesha. She was but one of a host of people prepared to leave their own homeland to serve in this particular part of the mission field. Not all came from Britain. There were doctors and nurses from Holland and Sri Lanka, from India and Japan, and from other parts of Africa, working with their Nigerian colleagues in a variety of roles.

It is the diversity of the people's skills in this book that is so impressive. There are the specialists whose achievements have won world wide renown. Dr David Morley's work as paediatrician, supported by the clinical skills of Sister Margaret Woodland, made possible the seminal child welfare project pioneered from Ilesha and now emulated in many parts of the world. But behind such a project, and indeed undergirding the whole work of the hospital, there has been the labour of countless technicians and clerks, builders and architects who have contributed their skills to the building of this hospital and its reputation. There are amazing, sometimes even amusing stories of the ways in which the Medical Suprintendent himself has had to act on occasions as accountant or architect, electrician or plumber, preacher or diplomat as well as doctor.

Dr Pearson, the longest serving Medical Superintendent at Ilesha, tells the hospital's story with typical modesty and total honesty. We are permitted to share both the joys and the agonies of the passing years. Those of us who have supported the work through the Wesley Guild can be thankful for all that has been accomplished in the hospital that still bears our name. Again, like all the best stories, this one leaves us guessing as to what happens next. But it ends with some clues as to how we can still be of 'one heart and one way' with those in Nigeria who continue to care for the sick in Christ's name today.

Pauline M. Webb.

A SECOND FOREWORD — FROM NIGERIA

Prof. R.O.A. Makanjuola, B.Sc., M.B. B.S., M. Phil., Ph.D., MRCPsych., FMCPsych., FWACP (Psych.)

Chief Medical Director
Obafemi Awolowo University
Teaching Hospitals Complex

Andrew Pearson directed the affairs of the Wesley Guild Hospital, Ilesha for twenty-three years (1952–1975), critical years which saw Nigeria's transition from colonial rule to independence, and latterly the take-over of the hospital by the government. He is in a unique position to write the history of the institution. He begins with the arrival of Dr J.R.C.Stephens in 1912, and the building of the old hospital between 1913 and 1915. He describes in detail the building of the new hospital and the move thence in 1954 (he was there!) and really ends with the traumatic events surrounding the take-over by the Western State government in 1975. He gives some information on the significant events thereafter. The Wesley Guild Hospital is the centre-piece of this book, but it also describes something of the Methodist Circuit medical work in the area which reached as far as Ekiti-land. The Imesi-Ile project is given deserved prominence. Dr Pearson's story is comprehensive, accurate and objective. Those of us who know what actually occurred at the time of the government take-over had good reason to expect that he would paint a very grim picture of the behaviour of our people at that time. The facts are that Dr and Mrs Pearson, and some other dedicated health workers, both missionary and Nigerian, were treated disgracefully. If anything, Dr Pearson plays down the episode, and there is no bitterness either in the book or in his personal interactions with us since then - a truly Christian attitude.

This story is about history, about medicine, even about adventure. Above all it is about dedication and sacrifice. All those who are interested in the history of Medicine in Nigeria, or about the history of Ijeshaland, should read this book. To those who do not fall into any of the above categories, the book is not just an academic narrative. It is also a very enjoyable read.

R.O.A.M.

Map of West Africa and South-West Nigeria

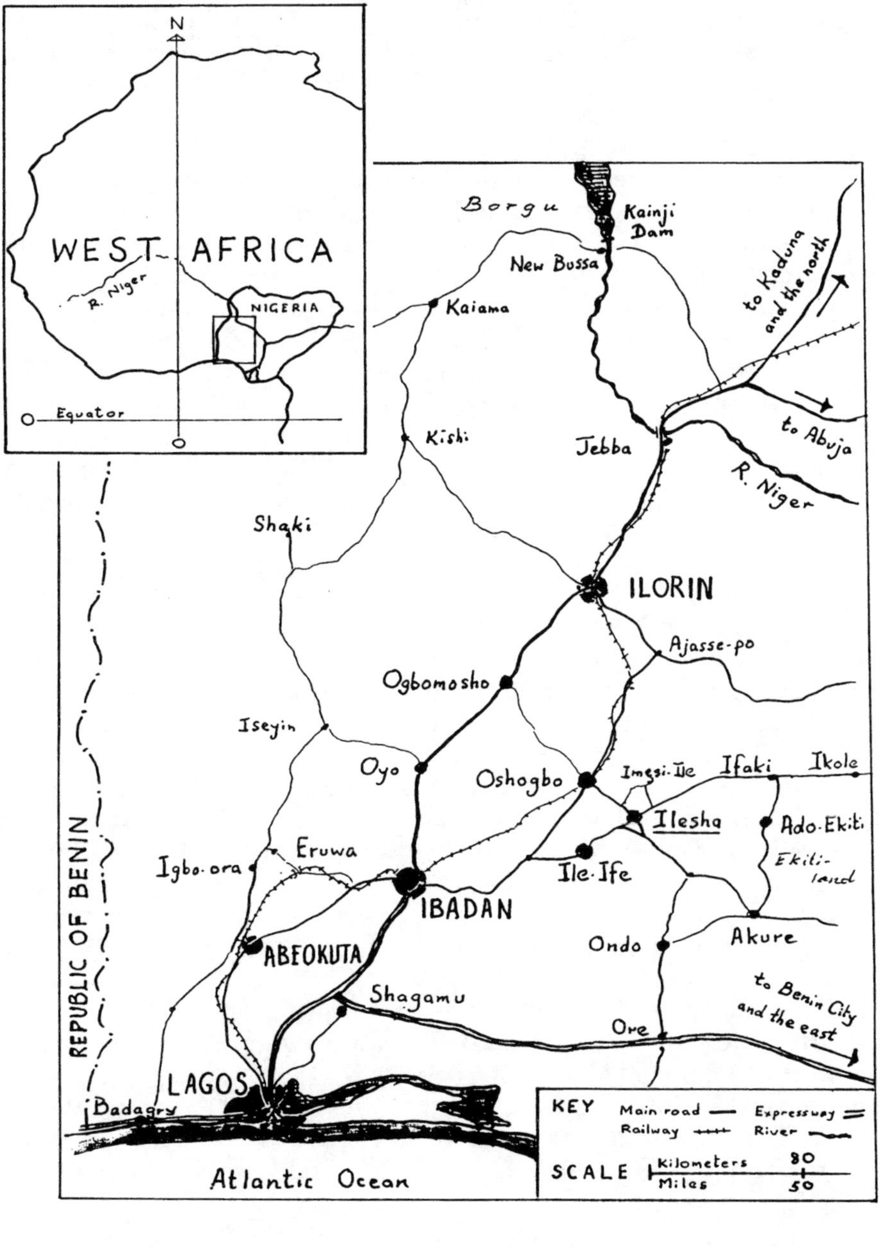

PREFACE

A visitor to Ilesha in south-west Nigeria will find a busy market town with a population of around 100,000, on the northern fringe of the rain forest 165 miles from the coast. The town was once on the main road from Lagos, the old capital and main port, inland through the city of Ibadan, then on via Akure and Benin to Onitsha, the gateway to the east. More direct routes to the eastern States have now been built, and Ilesha bypassed, but its importance not seriously diminished. The sturdy independence of the Ijesha people, a branch of the Yorubas who account for 95% of those who live in the area, is unchanged. Farming is still a major occupation. People tend to live in the town and commute out to their farms where they grow cocoa and food crops. Gold was once found in the rocky outcrops and streams around and forty prospectors filed their claims in the 1940's 'Ilesha gold rush'. By the 1950s the surface mines were no longer sufficiently productive, though the odd piece of quartz containing specks of gold could still be found. Only one miner, Johnny Passman, remained. The main modern industry is International Breweries run by Lawrence Omole, local business tycoon and philanthropist. His Trophy beer goes all over the country and beyond.

Drive to the centre of the town and ask any of the older members of the community the way to 'Wesley Guild Hospital' and they will direct you unhesitatingly down the main road towards Ibadan, then left up the hill of Ijofi Street to the roundabout at the top. The gate of a large hospital is there, but the name is different. 'OAUTHC' it says, meaning 'Obafemi Awolowo University Teaching Hospital Complex'. However, the original name is added, and the Guild badge is displayed for all to see. This is it. It is not, of course, where the work began. The 'old hospital site', on other side of the town has largely been forgotten. Even the old arched gateway has gone, though the original doctor's house, perched up on stilts, remains, defying the ravages of termites and time.

In 1975 the Wesley Guild Hospital, known to Ijesha people by that name since its inception in 1913, was taken over by decree by the Federal Government of Nigeria to be part of the teaching hospital complex for the new medical school at Ile-Ife twenty miles away. The original name was retained, partly to distinguish it from the three other hospitals initially in the complex, the Ife State Hospital, the Ife Seventh Day

Adventist Hospital, and the Ilesha Government General Hospital. It was retained also because of the good reputation the name carried throughout the country and beyond, and because of the affection with which it was known to the Ijesha people. They did not always understand what the 'Wesley Guild' name meant, and letters were sometimes received there addressed to 'Wesley Guide Hospital' or even 'Wesley Guita Hospital'!

There is a story behind that name, of course. Living witnesses in Britain and Nigeria of how it all began 83 years ago are now few, if any. It is time for the story to be written telling of the ups and downs of the early years, the crises and the successes as the institution became established, the work on the old site on the Ijebu-Jesha road, and on the present one at Ijofi, and the contributions to good health care for the nation, and indeed for the world, under its founding church proprietors. It began as a front-line hospital in terms of church outreach and medical pioneering in Africa. It continued to be in the front-line in nurse training, community child care innovation and in recognition as one of the best district level hospitals in the country That heritage has not been forgotten and much has been retained during the last twenty years in the hospital's new role under the university.

For the founders it is an opportune time because the Wesley Guild movement, which began within the Methodist Church in Britain in 1896, is celebrating its Centenary. Its long association with Ilesha hospital, and other hospitals in Nigeria and in Sierra Leone, Cote d'Ivoire and Kenya, are evidence of its special concern and support for the healing ministry of the Church world-wide. Among them all, Wesley Guild Hospital Ilesha was the first, and remained the flag-ship. So much giving and prayer had gone towards its support. At the height of the hand-over crisis at Ilesha in 1975, a missionary friend of the hospital from the Apostolic Church in Ilesha town, the late Pastor Elton, was talking with some members of the hospital staff. He had already been forty years in the country. He knew the people. He knew much of the hospital's history, and he made what I believe was a perceptive prophecy, 'There has been too much prayer for this place.' he said. 'The hospital cannot die'.

In part fulfilment, this book is written. We should keep on praying.

C. Andrew Pearson, February 1996.

ACKNOWLEDGEMENTS

Help has been obtained from many sources:

Ilesha and Beyond by Arthur E.Southon, Cargate Press, London, 1932. Rev Southon was the Methodist minister in Ilesha Circuit from 1912, and provides a vivid history of the hospital up to 1931.

A Hundred Years in Nigeria by F.Deaville Walker FRGS, Cargate Press, London, 1942. Written for the Methodist Church centenary, 1842–1942. Includes detail about the founding of the hospital.

A History of the Nigerian Health Services, by Dr Ralph Schram. Ibadan University Press, 1971. A mine of information.

In the Service of the Kingdom by Jonathan Clement; a biography of Dr E A Hunter, Medical Superintendent at Ilesha 1929–1941; written while the author was a medical student at the London Hospital. Wellcome Institute for the History of Medicine, 1994.

Methodism in Nigeria by church historian M.M.Familusi NPS Educational Publishers, Ibadan, Nigeria, 1992. A brief synopsis of the hospital's history brings the story up to date.

Mr Familusi's unpublished manuscript *History of Wesley Guild Hospital, Ilesa,* 1962, was obtained when this book was in final draft form. It was helpful in checking some of the facts.

Annual reports to the Methodist Missionary Society, 1920–1940, and *Numerical Returns* of work done 1917–1974.

Bi-annual *Wesley Guild Hospital Reports,* 1956–1974/5.

Old files, personal letters and other correspondence.

The help and advice of many former colleagues and friends is acknowledged with sincere thanks. These include:

Donald Campbell, David Cannon, Leslie Crosby, M.M.Familusi, Roland Hughes, Tunde Kuteyi, William Leary, Elsie Ludlow, Joyce and Nelson

Ludlow, Roger Makanjuola, David Morley, John Powell, John Pritchard, Howard Souster, Jack Souster, Pauline Webb, Bryan Pearson and Alison Marsh.

His Eminence Sunday Mbang, Prelate of the Methodist Church Nigeria, has seen the draft and kindly given the book his support.

So far as possible the history is given accurately and objectively. Where personal letters and memories are the source, and the account written in the first person, bias is likely to creep in. Please allow for that. Better some bias perhaps than an impersonal dullness!

So many people, both from Nigeria and from overseas, were involved in the story, and inevitably the contribution that some have made has not been included. My apologies to those whose names do not appear. It has been a major task, long waiting to be finished. So, thanks to all.

And special thanks to Joan Wright who would not let my conscience rest till the job was done!

C.A P.

Notes on spellings, pronunciation and abbreviations

The proper Yoruba spelling of Ilesha is 'Ilesa', with a dot under the 's' signifying an 'sh' sound in English spelling. In Nigeria the Yoruba spelling is naturally the preferred form, but for the assistance of the printer, and the convenience of non-Yoruba readers, the Anglicised spelling will be used in this book, as it was in the first 83 years of the hospital's history. The author begs forgiveness from the current Nigerian readers. Even when spelt 'Ilesha' the name has been commonly mispronounced overseas. The 'i' is short as in 'bit', and the 'e' is like an 'a' as in 'day'. Think of it as 'ill-Asia'.

'Ife' is pronounced 'Ee-fe' with the 'e' short as in 'fend'. The full name for the town is 'Ile-Ife', pronounced 'Ee-lay-Ee-fe', but the shorter form is used in speech, and often used in the text here. The abbreviation of 'University of Ife' to 'Unife' is common usage. The current name of

'Obafemi Awolowo University' (OAU), and OAU Teaching Hospital Complex (OAUTHC) is explained in the latter part of the book.

Guild supporters in Britain often referred to the Wesley Guild Hospital as 'Ilesha', not realising that was really the name of the town. While there was only the one hospital, that did not seem to matter. Now there are two, and also many run by private practitioners. For convenience, in the text, the full name 'Wesley Guild Hospital, Ilesha' is often abbreviated to 'WGH Ilesha', or, where appropriate the simple 'Ilesha' is still used.

During the course of the history there were several changes in Methodist nomenclature, both in Britain and Nigeria. These have largely been ignored in favour of 'the Methodist Church in Britain' or 'the Methodist Church Nigeria', for the sake of non-Methodist readers.

The Methodist Missionary Society (MMS) was the Wesleyan Methodist Missionary Society (WMMS) until 1932, when the Wesleyan, United and Primitive Methodist Churches came together as one Methodist Church.

For a time the Wesley Guild organization became the Methodist Guild, but a return was soon made to the familiar name. The MMS became the Methodist Church Overseas Division (MCOD) when the church was restructured in 1973, but it was a few years before the familiar 'MMS' was dropped from the letter-head, and from common use.

In Nigeria, west of the River Niger, it was the WMMS responsible for pioneering, and the church established was the Western Nigeria District of the Wesleyan Methodist Church in Britain. After 1932 it became the Western Nigeria District of the Methodist Church in Britain. There was an Eastern Nigeria District too, pioneered by the Primitive Methodist Church, and each District had its own Synod. After the granting of autonomy in 1962 both Districts were combined under one Conference of the 'Methodist Church Nigeria' (MCN). In 1976, under a new constitution taking episcopy into the MCN, the Districts became Dioceses.

The Hospital Management Committee is at times abbreviated to 'HMC'. The West African Council of Medical Research is denoted by its initials 'WACMR'

CHAPTER 1

PIONEERING YEARS, 1912–1928

The beginning of medical work in Ilesha was not so different from the start-up of any such work in a new area of a developing country today; find a doctor, decide the best location for serving the people in the area, ask for land on which to build, secure financial resources, buy the essential drugs and equipment, then get down to it. Ilesha Hospital's beginning followed roughly that pattern, but the early records make it sound very special. What is the justification?

Undoubtedly, there were special features. The Methodist Church had never recruited a doctor for anywhere in the entire continent of Africa before. It was not uncommon for the wives of missionary ministers to dress wounds and give out simple medicines to those who came to their back door for help. Some simple medical work had been pioneered by the 'Joyful News evangelist' John Bond, a lay missionary who had been in the country ten years before he was given a little basic health care training. He had then set up a clinic in the town of Igbo-Ora, twenty miles north of Abeokuta on the invitation of a traditional healer/herbalist who had become a Christian. Bond built a mud-walled dispensary (the ruins of which are still there today), and showed what could be done with minimal resources and skill, and much loving care. In other parts of the world the Methodist Missionary Society (MMS) had appointed doctors to the missionary team of ministers and educationists, beginning with one sent to Wuhan in China in 1864. Why not go further in Nigeria and build on what Bond had started?

Medical services were at an early stage in Nigeria. In a country four times the size of Britain there were by 1912 only eight hospitals (excluding the isolation centres for small-pox or leprosy). Five were government general hospitals (Calabar, Port Harcourt, Enugu, Sapele and Opobo) and three were mission hospitals - Sacred Heart Hospital, Abeokuta (Catholic) 1895, Itu Hospital (Presbyterian) 1906, and Iyi Enu Hospital,

Onitsha (Anglican) 1907. The Methodist initiative was about to produce a ninth hospital for the country. All this was in the year before Dr Albert Schweitzer gave up his career as philosopher, theologian, and musician, to devote himself to medical work in Africa. He arrived in Lambarene, Gabon in July 1913, and his dramatic move was to bring the work of the missionary doctor to the attention of the world.

Dr J.R.C. Stephens, 1912–1917

First Wesley Guild doctor

John R.C.Stephens, of Exmouth, England, who trained as a pharmacist and later as a doctor, had offered his services to the MMS in London. The Wesley Guild movement, within the Methodist Church in Britain had decided to support a medical mission in Africa, and the MMS approved. Dr Stephens was overwhelmed at finding himself selected to be the first 'Guild Doctor'. His personal and travel costs were guaranteed, and some essential start-up drugs and equipment provided. He, and his wife Nellie (Minifie), sailed from England in March 1912, and after two weeks arrived off the bar at Lagos, the main port for Nigeria. There they and their loads were precariously transhipped by surf-boat into land. It was only later that the harbour was dredged, and liners were able to enter and tie up at the Marina wharf on Lagos island to unload.

Igbo-Ora

The location for Guild medical work had still not been finally decided, but Dr and Mrs Stephens went first to Igbo-Ora, to relieve the Bonds who were due for leave. The journey was by the railroad which had been completed through to the interior and as far as Jebba on the Niger in the north of Nigeria only three years before (1909). At Sanusi station sixty-five miles up the line, they left the train and trekked the last twelve miles by bush-path, with carriers to bring loads on their heads. They settled in to the Bond's house and work began. There was no shortage of patients to see, and in six months Stephens treated 1700 in the dispensary, and cycled over 700 miles by bush path to people's homes and neighbouring villages. The people were happy, but some of the traditional healers and leaders of the Oro cult were less pleased with the competition. Dr Stephens became totally convinced that he must have a proper hospital into which patients could be admitted if treatments were to be effective and more lives saved.

Towards the end of that year the decision was taken by the Methodist Synod to make Ilesha the location. The church there was strong, and the local king, the Owa-Obokun of Ijeshaland, had himself become a Christian. The community was ready to welcome a doctor. Furthermore the town was connected to the new railway by a motor road to Oshogbo, 20 miles distant, completed in 1910. Lorries plied the road - early models with solid tyres! There was no motor road out of Lagos beyond Agege, 10 miles inland, because of the surrounding lagoons and mangrove swamps, and this was still the case, at least until 1927. A good transport facility was essential if there was to be a proper hospital, so - Ilesha it was to be, not Igbo-Ora.

Introduction to Ilesha

Dr and Mrs Stephens arrived on Jan 12th 1913. There was no house for them so they were given a room in the Nigerian minister's manse. The Rev. Arthur Southon, author of the book *Ilesha and Beyond*, who was still single, moved to live in the church vestry. Many patients, having heard that a doctor was coming, were waiting for Stephens in the church compound, including some with leprosy. He did what he could under a palm-leaf shelter. There is a picture of him performing an operation on a church bench outside the vestry, with his wife, who was not a nurse, and Mark, their house steward, as assistants. Search for land on which to begin building a hospital took time. After a long delay the Owa, 'mightily impressed', as Southon puts it, by the healing of a woman from his own palace, sanctioned a site outside the town defence ditch, away from other buildings. The Stephens hoped this would be sufficiently away from the persistent night-time drumming which did not help their sleep! The church members themselves set to clear bush from the eight acres. The agreed pepper-corn rent was one penny per year, but it was not until 1917 that the actual deeds for the land appeared, duly signed by the Governor-General Sir Frederick (later Lord) Lugard himself.

Towards the end of 1913 Dr Stephens and his wife went on leave. It was the practice of the MMS to insist on six months furlough (that is, leave) after an eighteen month tour of duty. In other countries longer tours were allowed, but not in West Africa, which was considered, with good reason, to be particularly hazardous to health. The six months was not just holiday leave. It was expected that at least half the time would be spent visiting churches and other groups to talk about the mission overseas, to raise awareness and encourage giving. Dr Stephens made a point of appealing to the Guilds for more money. He knew the need now first hand. He also ordered an entire prefabricated house for immediate dispatch. It was made of wood and asbestos sheet, with corrugated iron roof and standing on steel girders six feet from the ground. Dr R Schram records that such houses were common in Lagos, and were usually dispatched from England together with six artisans, and the planks for three coffins! The use of local timber and the training of sawyers had not yet begun. The coffin planks were probably the ones Dr Hunter found unused when he arrived in 1929. Fear of 'the white man's grave' was in retreat, as the dangers of untreated malaria, yellow fever and other diseases began to be understood and controlled.

Dr Stephens returned in 1914 to supervise the house building on the site outside the town wall on the Ijebu-Jesha bush-path, and also a mud-walled waiting hall to seat righty, with side-rooms for consulting and three-beds. Building progress was painfully slow, but he was encouraged when a missionary nurse, Gwladys Charlesworth (she used the Welsh spelling for her first name), was sent to join him in 1915. Her church donated a portable operating table. The new buildings were officially opened on Jan 8th 1916, and that year the hospital, which was really only a dispensary, recorded over 10,000 out-patient attendances, 200 operations, forty-five in-patients and seven deliveries, with a total staff of seven. The first motor road from Ibadan to Ilesha was completed in 1917, and Ilesha was to become an important centre of communications.

Set-backs

As the 1914–18 Great War in Europe dragged on, there was an inevitable falling off of contributions from the Guilds, and the value of the pound dropped to a third of its pre-war level. Dr Stephens was left with no resources, and with no possibility of turning the dispensary into a proper hospital. After five years of struggle and an immense amount of work, he decided he could be better used elsewhere, and accepted an invitation to work with the government at their hospital in Ilorin, where he stayed many years. Because of the war no doctor was available to replace him, so in mid-1917 the centre at Ilesha was closed. Initial hopes were dashed. Weeds took over in the compound.

Sister Charlesworth went to Lagos to stay at the Methodist Girls High School temporarily, and when travelling home was on the same boat as a missionary minister, the Rev. John Stewart. The 1918 pandemic of

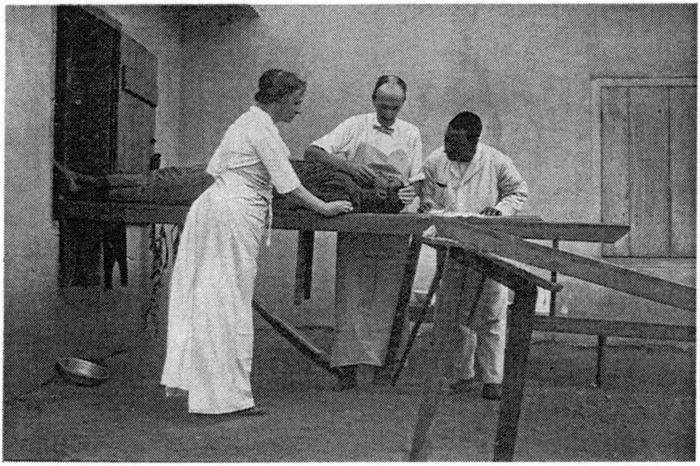

Fig 1.1 *The first operation*

Fig 1.2 *Dr Stephens' bungalow*

Asian influenza swept through Nigeria, causing as many deaths as elsewhere in the world. Some blamed the white men for introducing it. John Stewart at this time was back on his own in Ifaki, an even more rural posting than Ilesha. Assassins were detailed to kill him in order to save the village. The day the deed was to be done, John fell sick with the flu himself, and was unconscious for five days. His attackers came that night, looked through the window of his house and seeing him ill went away. If the 'flu had affected him, they reasoned, he could not be the cause. When John finally regained consciousness, it was to see his steward grinning at him through the window, amazed that he had recovered. By now the plot was common knowledge, and John discovered the flu had saved his life! Gwladys Charlesworth came out again, married John Stewart in 1919 at Tinubu Church in Lagos, and went to share the life in Ekiti, and contribute her skills in health promotion.

The minister in Ilesha from November 1916 was the Rev. Leonard F. Webb, who had just arrived in the country and was on his first posting. After the closure of the hospital he was appalled at the sufferings of the people. In his diary he recalled a women dying in obstructed labour while her husband remained fatalistically indifferent. During most of the 1918 flu epidemic the Rev. Webb was away on leave, but returned and served till 1922, becoming a fluent Yoruba speaker. His youngest daughter, Pauline, born five years later, was to become a well-known Christian leader, journalist and broadcaster, and in 1965 the Vice-President of Conference of the Methodist Church in Britain, and a Vice-President of the World Council of Churches too. On a visit to Ilesha in 1974 she made a presentation of an item of medical equipment to WGH in memory of her father. The Church warmly recalled his work at a Circuit Rally.

Dr Edward U. MacWilliam, 1920–1928

A fresh start

When the war was over, and soldiers returned home, a replacement doctor became available. Dr E. U. MacWilliam, an Irishman, arrived in mid 1920, and surveyed the neglected mud-walled 'so-called hospital' and doctor's house. Weeds were cleared, buildings cleaned and re-painted and the centre reopened for business. Mark Okunsanya, Dr

Fig 1.3 *The main ward block, built by Dr MacWilliam*

Fig 1.4 *The gatehouse, symbol of the hospital to many overseas supporters, and used in the design of the front cover of Southon's book, published 1932*

Stephen's former helper, was appointed medical assistant. Patients began to reappear, and numbers rapidly escalated. It was clear to Dr MacWilliam that a second doctor was needed to cover when the first was away on leave, also nursing sisters to train local helpers. He drew up plans for more staff housing, and a proper hospital with a two-storey ward for men downstairs, and for women and children upstairs, a larger out-patient department, operating theatre, laboratory and pharmacy. A Secretarial visit from MMS, London, confirmed the importance of this opportunity, and the Guilds were once more inspired to raise the money to make their dream of a Medical Mission come true. Building began in earnest.

After Dr MacWilliam's first leave he was joined in 1922 by Sister Stella Liony, a black British nurse born in London. Her father, a Yoruba man, died young, and she was brought up by her God-fearing mother, who was of Danish origin. While at a Methodist Church in east London, she heard a call to devote herself to serve her father's people in Africa, so trained as a nurse and midwife. Her contribution in Ilesha was to be of an importance which it would be difficult to exaggerate. She quickly became fluent in Yoruba language, and persuaded local families to allow their girls to come to the hospital for nurse training. This was a breakthrough. Male-nurses were still the rule in government service. By 1923 twelve beds were in use, and this had risen to twenty-four by 1925, when a second doctor, Dr T C Lonie, and a second nurse, Miss G. L. Baker, joined the team. After one tour (1925–1927) Dr Lonie retired with sickness, and a Dr G Lowe came, only to move to government service after nine months. Sister A. McKnight arrived to help, and the wards were generally served by two sisters and 4 nurses in training. There were ante-natal clinics for expectant mothers, and a welfare clinic for babies in their first year. More housing was added in 1926 and also the gatehouse lodge, with its arched entrance, the picture of which became well known in Britain as a symbol of the hospital.

By 1927 there were 27,000 out-patient attendances a year, 450 operations and thirty-five deliveries. A leprosy settlement was started on some unused, rather swampy land, on the lowest part of the hospital site. The patients grew vegetables, and received a small cash allowance from the hospital. It was to be nine years before better land could be found for them.

Hopes dashed again

The hospital appeared to be on its way to becoming securely established, but hopes of a permanent second doctor faded with the departure of Dr Lowe. There was a further set-back at the end of 1928 when the MacWilliams had to leave precipitately because their two year-old son, John, became severely ill with dysentery. They had no doctor to hand over to, and were disheartened, feeling that 'the work of years was falling about their ears like a pack of cards'. Nevertheless, as the Methodist Synod appreciation of Dr MacWilliam put it,

> 'During his eight years service he has seen the hospital develop from a mud dispensary to an efficient institution'.

Progress had been made.

Sister Liony and Sister McKnight carried on themselves for seven months, doing good work and successfully treating a son of the powerful neighbouring supreme chief or king, the Oni of Ife. Then they too were due for leave, and in July 1929 the hospital had to be closed once more. There was no replacement doctor till October. For another wet season the grass grew unchecked.

CHAPTER 2

STEADY GROWTH, AND PREPARATION FOR A MOVE, 1929–1952

Dr Hunter, 1929–1941

A new beginning
The coming of Dr Edward A Hunter in October 1929 brought fresh hope to the Guild project, and his twelve years at Ilesha were indeed a period of remarkable progress. He had graduated with honours from the London Hospital Medical College in 1929, coming top of all the medical students in London University. As a committed Christian, he hoped to go as a medical missionary to South China where his future father-in-law, Dr Webb Anderson had pioneered medical work in Foshan (formerly Fatshan), but he was to be disappointed. Faced with the staff crisis in Ilesha, the MMS appointed Dr Hunter to Nigeria - and there he went. It was two years before he completed his probation, as the MMS then required, and he could return to marry his fiancee, Doris Anderson.

Nurse training
Stella Liony, the pioneer in Nigeria of female nurse training, returned with Dr Hunter, and was joined in December 1929 by Sister Elsie Ludlow who was to stay for 31 years, and make as great a contribution as Stella. Initially they had only three part-trained nurses, one male dresser in OPD, and an untrained male aid on for nights. In 1931 it was decided that two female nurses should go on night duty to provide better care. The girls had a great fear of darkness, and one objected to a night shift so strongly that she left. Two were willing to put the care of patients before their fears, and their example ensured that there was never any further difficulty in arranging for night duty.

Nurses had a natural fear of contracting disease from their patients, and of some diseases in particular. One man with leprosy came each day to have a sore on his foot dressed, and he was always left for sister to do. The nurses were 'too afraid'. Elsie recalls that one day she was delayed, and on reaching the OPD asked where the patient was.

'Yes, he came,' said one nurse, 'but he had to wait too long, so I have done his dressing'. In small ways their natural fears were gradually overcome.

Elsie also remembers talking to a chief in a village who had been admitted one night with a strangulated hernia, and saved through an emergency operation. As a result of his time in hospital he became a Christian, not, he said, because of what he had heard from the nurses in ward prayers, but by the way they did their work. Their tasks were sometimes difficult, even objectionable, and their hours long, but they worked willingly and cheerfully. He could see that they could not do it without help, and when he found their help came from God, he decided he needed God too. He held a Thanksgiving Service in his village church when he returned.

A new three-year training programme in both nursing and midwifery was drawn up, and arrangements made for a Hospital Certificate to be awarded to those passing the final examination. The first candidate, Nurse Emily, passed in 1932, and the Wesley Guild Hospital badge, with its motto 'One Heart, One Way', was ready for presentation. It has since been given to every nurse qualifying at WGH.

From 1932 the midwifery training was accepted for the government's Grade II Midwifery Certificate, but with the stipulation that mothers and babies had to be nursed in hospital for 5 days after delivery. The custom had been for one day only, and it took quite a battle to persuade the mothers, and the fathers, that this was necessary! In 1934 Nurse Emily was the first WGH candidate to pass the Grade II Midwifery examination, and Bernice Falaye was the first Midwife to pass the hospital's Nursing Certificate examination. From 1939 the government service recognized the Hospital Certificate in nursing, and the numbers coming for training increased. National nursing qualifications and Grade I Midwifery were still to come. Stella Liony and Elsie Ludlow worked very well together. Both had a good sense of humour, and enjoyed fun with the nurses, and their friends in the town. Elsie recalls that Stella was always saying 'First things first'. She really did place God's will uppermost in all she did.

Sister Elsie Moody came in 1930, and was encouraged by Stella Liony to make the hospital the first in Nigeria to organize a kitchen to feed in-patients. Patients' relatives had to bring food in all other hospitals. In 1938 she was moved to pioneer new work in Ifaki, Ekiti, for a further three years. Many others sisters and doctors followed as the years went by.

Edward Hunter married his fiancee Doris in Sept 1931 in London, with the great Rev. Donald (later, Lord) Soper performing the ceremony. Three weeks after coming out to Nigeria she nearly died of a serious malaria attack, being at death's door for six weeks. She was saved only by Edward giving her quinine intra-muscularly, because she could not keep it down orally. Subsequently she surprised other expatriates of her day by bringing up her children in Nigeria. She was a trained nurse herself and helped the hospital Sisters by running a 'Prelim' course in basic nursing for the students, teaching medical terms, dressings technique, temperature taking etc., but did not feel she deserved to be called 'the first sister tutor'. The two doctors gave twelve medical lectures a week between them. Training nurses for the country was a major concern of the hospital then, and it has remained so for the last 60 years.

Support grows

Despite the serious economic depression in Britain in the early 1930s the Guilds in Britain were expanding fast, and reached their zenith in 1934 with 175,000 senior members and over 50,000 juniors in 5000 branch meetings. Another Guild Hospital in Sierra Leone was given support from 1930. In 1931 money was donated by the London branches of the Guild, and used to build a good operating theatre at Ilesha in memory of one their great leaders, the Rev. Francis C.Ream. The 'RMT' (Ream Memorial Theatre) was opened in July 1932, and the first operation performed by Dr Hunter and Dr Woods jointly was on a patient with double hernia, a surgeon to each side, so that both could share the honour! 'RMT' was to remain the theatre's name, even after transfer to the new site. In 1932 a new Nurses' Home was completed, and there were 10 nurses in residence receiving training.

Efforts were made to achieve a degree of local self-sufficiency. Whereas missionary salaries were covered from overseas, the policy was to meet running expenses from fees. Costs for the patients were kept as low as possible, 6d for medicine, 2/6d for an injection and 30/- for a hernia repair, inclusive of three weeks in hospital. Those unable to pay were treated free.

The first grant from the Nigerian government, £950, was used to install a small diesel generator and electric light, a novelty at that time in Ilesha. The official switching-on was performed by the Owa, with gasps of admiration from the crowds as the hospital was flooded with light!

The Methodist Church in Nigeria gave increasing support through annual collections on 'Hospital Sunday', which began about 1933. There was also support from the Guild movement which spread to churches in Nigeria. The Methodist Boys High School, Lagos, raised money every year. Such support was significant because it came in the face of a rise of belief in miraculous divine healing. Ilesha was the very centre from which the Joseph Babalola movement started. Joseph, who had been a Public Works Department road roller driver, suddenly started public preaching in the open air, and claiming powers of healing. Thousands of sick came from all over the country. Ilesha was besieged. Hospital attendance dropped by twenty-five per cent at the start, but the 'competition' did not last for long and patient numbers soon rose again, some coming from as far afield as Port Harcourt and Timbuktu! Dr Hunter said he saw little hard evidence of miracles, but the Apostolic Church, with a divine healing emphasis, grew out of the religious revival. The Methodist Church supported the mission hospital approach which was to show God's love to all in need, and use every method God had provided, be it medicine, surgery - or prayer.

It is true, the facilities which the staff had available were still very simple. Many years later, at the hospital's Fiftieth Jubilee in 1962 Dr Hunter recalled:

> 'There was no running water, bush-lamps only for operating room and wards, and primus-stove sterilisation. There was no laboratory, no antibiotics or intravenous therapy. Digitalis and brandy were the best we could do for pneumonia. We had quinine and emetine, but not much else of curative value. Anaesthesia was by chloroform, or

spinal. Surprisingly people got better in fair numbers, and the work grew rapidly, especially in surgery, midwifery and infant welfare. The type of practice was the same as now, with tropical infections, trauma and hernias our chief preoccupation.....Letters, accounts, wages, drains, buildings etc were all part of the doctor's duties.'

Outreach

Dr Helena Gambrell came for the first half of 1931, standing in for Dr Joyce Woods who should have come but needed time to complete her studies and qualify as a surgeon, FRCS (London). She arrived in July, but it was to be the obstetric rather than the surgical calamities which first grabbed her attention. She was appalled by the high maternal and infant mortality that she found. Her first four maternity patients taught her a lesson. The first was brought dead, and the second and third died shortly after arrival before treatment could be given. The fourth had been so long in labour she had a still-birth, and then a vesico-vaginal fistula. Only from the fifth did she emerge with a live child and a live mother, though a three-day labour also resulted in a fistula. All the mothers were coming too late. She resolved to start visiting villages, holding ante-natal clinics and picking up the problems early.

Dr Hunter came too when he could, especially to areas where yaws was very prevalent, causing sores and deformity. Three injections of the arsenical, Acetylarsan, gave a miraculous-seeming cure, and some say this early exposure to 'the needle' was the origin of the exaggerated belief in injected drugs which has continued to this day! It was about this time that Dr Hunter was given the nick-name 'Ayarabiasha', meaning 'Swift as a hawk', perhaps because he used a bicycle down the bush-paths when visiting villages. Years before, around 1912, when the Rev. Oliver Griffin the District Chairman had used the first bicycle ever seen in Ilesha, he was called by that same name.

In 1933 Dr Woods resigned to marry the Rev. Nelson Ludlow who had arrived in Ilesha to take charge of the Circuit. She moved across to the church compound, but came over to the hospital to help out part time. Now, as Dr Joyce Ludlow, she took the opportunity to travel with her husband on his pastoral work, and from 1934 to 1946 they developed a network of pioneer village health centres (dispensaries) offering primary care and maternity services to the people of Imesi-Ile, Ipetu-Ibokun, Oshu, Ijeda and Esa-Oke. All the centres were financed by the

Ilesha Circuit, and staffed by nurses given midwifery training at WGH or at Ilorin General Hospital where a Christian Matron was in charge, and most helpful. In 1936 the Ludlows went even further afield in the newly created Ilorin Circuit using their mobile dispensary. Mrs Wende Awoseyi, with her two children, went to Afon, just south of Ilorin city, to help establish the work, and Mrs Victoria Thompson (nee Agbosola) worked at Kaiama, in Borgu Division, fifty miles north of Ilorin, together with Stephen Oshiobugie the dispenser. Only in 1946, when the Ludlows moved away from Ilesha, were the Circuit centres adopted by WGH. Supervision of the Ilorin Circuit health work was taken on by the hospital when the Ludlows returned to England in 1952.

The very first of the health centres, built in 1934, was at Imesi-Ile, twenty-five miles from Ilesha on top of a mountain ridge. The people put up a little mud-walled clinic to the Rev. Ludlow's specification. Bernice Falaye, the first qualified nurse-midwife from WGH Ilesha, agreed to be stationed there, even though she had to walk the last ten miles through the bush carrying her midwifery bag. On her first night she was called out to a woman with severe post-partum bleeding in a hut five miles distant. She was frightened, but ran most of the way, and saved the patient's life. Thus from the beginning she had the villagers' confidence. The work grew, but it was five years before there were resources to build a proper maternity home at Imesi-Ile, with delivery room, treatment room and a large verandah as waiting area. In 1957 the Imesi-Ile centre was to be given a strategic new role in child health research, but nobody could foresee such developments in 1934!

Expansion

In 1934 Dr Donald M Beaugie arrived and proved an excellent colleague. Hospital work was never busier. In 1935 the hospital was expanded with a large new Men's Ward, Maternity Department, and a block for Kitchen, Laundry, Engine Room, and Doctor's Office. Bed-capacity of the hospital was now fifty-five. All water from roofs was ducted into a large underground tank from where it was pumped to a cistern in the men's ward roof. For the first time the hospital had running water.

Around that time a start was made in treating leprosy with sub-cutaneous injections of chaulmoogra oil, and the number of patients camping on the swampy land below the hospital increased dramatically. The new therapy perhaps did a little good, but patients remained shunned by society and without real hope. When on leave in 1935 Dr Hunter mentioned their problem to the British Leprosy Relief Association, and returned to Ilesha with £36 from them, and a resolve to build a worthy colony for the men. Three acres of land was acquired across the road from the hospital, and the doctors themselves worked with the patients to make bricks and mix concrete, and construct a circle of houses with their own hands. A small chapel constructed of stone was then added, with an unglazed arched window looking out towards Mount Imo to the north of Ilesha town. The cost of materials for the chapel was covered by a £50 gift from Elsie Moody's home church in Britain. Dr Beaugie wrote.

> 'The difference in the men would amaze you. Through service for their community they have come to learn something of the love of God, and there is a quite different spirit among them. Their physical condition too is greatly improved'.

Recognition

In February 1936 Ilesha town opened its new Town Hall. It had been built by the Welsh engineer of the Public Works Department, the inimitable Taffy Jones, said to be a member of the Ogboni secret society, who drove the first dual carriage-way through the city of Ibadan. This fine road, passing Ibadan's new city hall on the hill at Molete was nick-named 'Taffy's Highway'. For his work he was honoured by being the first European in Nigeria to be made a traditional chief. The second such chief was to come from Ilesha. At the official opening of its Town Hall the Owa-Obokun of Ijeshaland conferred a chieftaincy title on Dr Edward Hunter, making him the 'Oluawo of Ilesha', head of the medicine-men of the town. He knelt before the Owa to receive his chief's beads of office. He was the first missionary to be given such an honour.

Staff changes, and the stress of war-time

Dr Beaugie returned from his first furlough in 1936, having become engaged. Audrey arrived in February, and the wedding took place in Otapete Church, Ilesha. The Hunters then went for their leave, but Dr Beaugie unfortunately fell victim to amoebic dysentery so badly that he had to be repatriated in June. The Sisters had to cope until Dr and Mrs Hunter returned in September. Dr Gambrell, now Dr Pudney and living in Nigeria, came to help part-time, but it was not until 1938, that Dr Leslie Crosby arrived to work full-time, and to stay seven years (1938–1945).

1939 saw the outbreak of the Second World War, and communications between Nigeria and Britain became difficult. First beginnings were being made towards building up a locally appointed staff. In 1937 the church recommended one of their own members Mr James Balogun as interpreter, but he also learned the skills of microscopy, sufficient to run the small laboratory, and he assisted with anaesthetics. In 1940 he was joined by Mr Hezekiah Awodiya, a keen member of the church and of the Scouts. In addition to being interpreter, he was made first assistant in the operating theatre. Both men proved loyal members of staff and stayed until their retirement. Mr Awodiya eventually became Hospital Manager.

In 1940 Dr and Mrs Hunter decided the time had come to retire, but there was no ship that year, and no replacement available from the MMS. Because of the delay the doctors obtained a site on a hill three miles south of Ilesha, and built a small holiday bungalow where they could get away for a rest. The Hunters even cut the road up to it themselves. Mrs Hunter recalls a stay there with their first radio, and listening to the news of the Battle of Britain, which seemed so far away. However, it was probably not practical to maintain this retreat for such occasional use. Eventually, in September 1941, the Hunter family sailed on a cargo boat which took two months to reach Liverpool having had to go nearly to Newfoundland to avoid German submarines. Relatives had given them up for lost. By the 1950s the bungalow had been taken over by Johnny Passman, the gold-miner, with Queenie his wife, and I recall one visit to what was by then known as 'Passman's Hill', to see the bungalow, and mining shed with a primitive conveyor belt for separating the columbite and gold from the alluvial washings.

Dr John Powell, 1942–1952

Dr Crosby carried on for a year (1941–1942), as the lone doctor in residence, and was greatly relieved by the arrival of Dr John and Barbara Powell, in 1942, when he was at last able to go on leave. While John was on his next leave in 1944, Leslie asked for two months off to get married in Lagos and have a honeymoon. At short notice Dr Howard Souster, who had just completed a full and exhausting tour at Ituk Mbang Hospital, was asked if he would take over at Ilesha for the two months 'on his way home'. Though he quailed at the prospect he accepted partly because of the close relationship between his family and that of the Rev. Francis Ream who had christened him, and in whose memory the operating theatre at Ilesha had been built. He could not refuse! Dr Crosby was released for his wedding, and he and his wife returned home finally in 1945.

Howard had no idea in 1944 that in January 1947 his own brother, Dr Jack Souster, would be selected to provide the second medical member of the team working with John Powell. This was to be the only instance where two brothers served as missionaries at Ilesha, a rare distinction. Howard subsequently became a remarkably effective Medical Secretary of the Methodist Church Overseas Division, and later Vice-President of Conference.

From 1947 on there were never less than two full-time doctors at Ilesha. With this type of stable staffing the hospital progressed at an ever increasing pace. By that year, with sixty-five beds, the hospital recorded 44,000 out-patient attendances, 1800 in-patients, 620 operations and 560 deliveries. Probationer nurses were now up to twenty-one. James Balogun and Hezekiah Awodiya assisted the doctors on night calls to theatre, 'overtime unpaid on the same terms as missionary staff', as John Powell recalls,

> 'They had become friends and colleagues'.

When a patient came from Ibadan, seventy-five miles away, for operation John asked him why he had come to Ilesha, and not to the hospital near his home, and received the reply,

> 'Because you pray first'.

John mused, 'It does good to the medical man to be reminded of things spiritual in the midst of his medical and more material matters.'

A new site?

The first thoughts that the hospital was outgrowing its eight acres had, in fact, been voiced as early as 1945. The land was rather low-lying, with a mosquito-infested swamp on one side, and the 3-acre leprosy settlement on another. Further acquisition of adjacent land was impossible.

It was a visiting government Development Officer in 1947 who first positively advocated re-building on a new site. Dr Powell took this up with the Owa and the Divisional Officer for Ilesha, and the idea captured the imagination and enthusiasm of the 'progressive elements' in the town. John was even shown a 33-acre area of higher land at Ijofi outside the wall on the other side of Ilesha town. This seemed very suitable and discussions were taken to the church and mission authorities in Lagos and London. The Medical Secretary from MMS, Dr Ralph Bolton, visited in 1948. Dr Powell has a memory of him trying to climb a palm-tree, but giving up quickly when he barked his shin! He too joined the others in giving general approval, but there the matter rested for the time being.

Technology

In 1947 the first X-ray plant arrived, a 15-milliamp portable machine, a gift from the Guilds. A small X-ray room and dark-room was built for it. Mr Michael Abe was employed as the first radiography assistant. Mr S A Laniyan was the mechanic in charge of the generator engines, and other maintenance matters, ably assisted by Dr Powell who had the reputation of being a practical man. A visitor coming to the hospital was as likely to find him under the hospital lorry as in the operating room! Writing in 1950, and describing occasions when he had been called to an emergency in the generator room when the lights had failed, he waxed lyrical.

> 'Finding that spanners and hammers were of no further use in our manipulation of intricate engineering devices, recourse was made to the operating theatre for the more delicate instruments of the surgeon's art whereby to effect repair of the fuel pump or dynamo, twiddling a wire into place with Spencer-Wells artery forceps, or collecting a nut from some impossible position with a long Kocher's, followed at long last with success, and the pleasing result of light to gladden the night hours, and make possible the continued watch of doctor and nurse upon the sick and pain-filled folk who crowded our wards'.

He summed up the competencies of an Ilesha doctor with his usual dry humour by saying,

> 'He should be able to pass lightly from the intricacies of a diesel engine to the comparative simplicity of a gastro-enterostomy!'

A tragic loss precedes steps forward in nurse training

The Matron, Stella Liony, was very ill in 1946, with much pain and for several weeks her life was in the balance. Fortunately she recovered sufficiently to travel home to Britain in 1947. After twenty-five years of such devoted service, one can imagine how much she was missed. The people had called her 'Iya-agba' (Grandma) which was truly a sign of affection in the Yoruba culture.

Even though she could not return, news from Ilesha must have gladdened Stella's heart. In 1946 the Medical Board of the Christian Council of Nigeria was formed, and representatives of four missions with nurse training programmes met quarterly and drew up a more comprehensive nursing syllabus. They arranged for Inter-Mission nursing and midwifery examinations to be held twice a year. In 1948 Sister Enid Blake came out to join the nursing team. That same year the Nursing Council of Nigeria was inaugurated, and laid down regulations for a Nigerian Registered Nurse (NRN) qualification. Girls with Secondary Modern certificate would only have to do a six months Preliminary Training School (PTS). Standard VI girls would require a full year. In 1949 Deaconess Florence Cutler was transferred to the hospital to teach the academic subjects for PTS, and look after the students' welfare. In 1950 Sister Blake was released to study for the Sister Tutor's qualification in London. The intake of students that year was the first to be recognized for NRN, and the first to qualify were in 1954. It was about this time that the practice of calling nurses just by their first name was dropped. There were too many Graces, Comforts and Abigails, and the switch to surnames had to be made.

The primary care network

The out-station work at Ifaki and Ikole in the Ekiti area eighty miles away was by now staffed by a missionary sister, Miss Louie Trott, but the Ikole Maternity Hospital still required a doctor's visit once a month. The roads through the forest were often blocked by fallen trees, and the narrow wooden bridges were hazardous in the wet season, but Sister Trott was rarely deterred. Her name was difficult to translate into Yoruba so the Ekiti people called her 'Toro', which was the name of the three-penny bit then in circulation! They spoke the word with tongue-in-cheek and a smile around the lips, for Louie was anything but a 'bit'. She ran the 30-bed maternity hospital, with its staff of midwives and pupils, with strict rules, and woe betide visitors, be they ever so high and influential, if they came at the wrong time. They loved her nonetheless, and her impartial care for rich or poor, young or old, high or low, was a powerful witness for good. The people of Omuo-Ekiti, twenty miles east of Ikole, begged her to supervise a health centre and maternity home which they had built, and she stationed midwives there and carried the responsibility of supervision on her own.

The five centres in the Ilesha district, 15 to 25 miles distant, at Imesi-Ile, Esa-Oke, Ipetu, Oshu and Ijeda, were regularly visited by a doctor or health sister from Wesley Guild Hospital. There was in place the beginnings of what would now be called a 'District Health System', with a network of primary care clinics around a first-referral hospital. From Ilesha supervision was given to the midwives and helpers appointed to the villages, essential drugs were provided each month, and the hospital gave priority to their referred cases. When doctors or sisters visited they often brought serious cases back with them. Only environmental health matters were handled by the government's sanitary inspectors.

Plans for rebuilding

The debate about whether the hospital should be rebuilt on a new site was revived in 1950 when Dr Powell's leave was covered for a few months by Dr John Rose, who had formerly worked in China at the Fatshan Hospital where Dr Hunter had hoped to be appointed. John was of the opinion that the hospital should not move, but rather built upwards, as was becoming the common practice in China. However, the matter was settled at the Methodist Synod in Lagos that year, when the veteran missionary, the Rev. Bill Mellor, made a proposal that the hospital should be built by the Blaize Memorial Institute, Abeokuta, a Church Missionary Society centre for training carpenters, of which he was a member of the executive. If half the cost could be raised from grants and donations he said that up to £30,000 could be treated as a loan from Blaize repayable over ten years from the hospital's current income. That clinched it. Legal deeds for the leasehold of the thirty-three acres, at £1 per acre a year, were forthwith obtained. Dr Powell drew out sketch-plans for what the government called a 'country-type hospital' of 114 beds in single-storey buildings connected by covered ways. Mr Harry Jobling, a Methodist Local Preacher, was the manager/trainer at the Blaize. He costed the plans at £48,000. The Nigerian government agreed to pay a grant of £18,000, and to buy the site for £10,000 for use as a Divisional Teachers' Training College. The Ilesha Local Government agreed to raise £5000 over three years by raising a 1/- a year from each tax-payer. The Wesley Guilds and Methodist Youth Department in Britain promised £2500. Further donations from within Nigeria swelled the funds. All was agreed, the land at Ijofi was cleared except for the palm trees, and in December 1951 the first sod was cut by His Highness the Owa of Ijeshaland, Oba Ajimoko II, at an enthusiastic celebration and £1000 collected in donations on the spot! Building actually began, and in the dry months of January to March 1952 the first buildings went up made of compressed mid-brick. These were two of the utility buildings to act as stores for cement and timber (and protect them from the rain), and an office building in which Harry and his wife Nellie could live temporarily while on the job.

Dr and Mrs Powell then went home finally after completing ten years packed with incident and hope, leaving Dr Jack Souster in charge.

CHAPTER 3

REBUILDING, 1952–1954

Dr Pearson, 1952–1975

The heritage of forty years
From 1952 on, the story involves myself, and much will inevitably be told in the first person. My dates as Medical Superintendent of the hospital head this paragraph to bring things into line with the previous two chapters. The first forty years of the history have largely fallen into the periods when the pioneer senior doctors were in charge, Dr Stephens, Dr MacWilliam, Dr Hunter, Dr Crosby and Dr Powell. All the way through, of course, others played their part, matrons, sisters, medical colleagues for shorter or longer periods, and the church and community leaders who supported them. It was a team effort, and as more nurses were trained, and other local staff joined the team, so responsibility shifted to Nigeria, and to the Ilesha people in particular. It always was their hospital, with the land on which it was built leased to the church for medical use, and the people's backing given to the team in charge. The good service given was recognized. Though it carried the name of the 'Wesley Guild' it was never the Wesley Guild's property, just theirs to give for and pray for and assist in any way possible.

It was a privilege to be appointed to serve at the Ilesha Hospital which had such a high profile among Methodists in Britain because of the consistent support of churches, Guilds, Guild Holiday Homes and the MMS for forty years. Few church members were unaware of it. Many had given sacrificially and regularly throughout the hospital's existence, and they had extended their help to other centres too. A new hospital was opened in Segbwema, Sierra Leone in 1930, and a year or two later another at Ituk Mbang in Eastern Nigeria. Maua Hospital in Kenya followed. The healing ministry was accepted as an essential arm of the churches outreach in every part of the world, and for Guilders this area or missionary work had a special appeal. Support for the Ilesha Wesley Guild Hospital in 1952 was still strong.

So here we were, in April of that year. As it turned out, we saw the hospital through for the final twenty-three years of its history as a mission institution. Ilesha became our home until 1975.

China background

Previously Mrs Pearson and I had been in China with the MMS, part of the time at the Hospital of Universal Love, Hankow, the first Methodist hospital to be founded anywhere in the world. I went there in 1946, and Jean Frost, my fiancee, followed in 1948, and we were married in the hospital chapel. The Communist Revolution followed in 1949, and we stayed until 1951, when it became evident that anyone from the west was becoming more of an embarrassment than a help to our Chinese friends. We returned with our first child, Michael, born 1950. The second, Roger, was born three weeks after our boat from Hong Kong arrived in England - a close run thing!.

During my five years in China, apart from learning the language, I had done mainly surgery, under the tuition of Chinese surgeons, but also general medicine and leprology. I had done no obstetrics, and no hospital administration. In my last year I had worked at the big Union Hospital in Wuhan, with a team of 18 doctors under a consortium of missions, It was taken over by the new health authorities, combined with two other hospitals and made into a medical university, run efficiently by over a hundred doctors without any help from overseas. On arrival in London I went to the offices of MMS to discuss what next. The Medical Secretary, Dr Bolton, said they would like me to take a nine-month break, and then go to Nigeria to be Medical Superintendent at Ilesha. In my innocence I asked how many doctors I would have working with me, imagining quite a big team for such a well-known hospital.

> 'You must be joking' he said, 'there will just be yourself, and one other'.

So, we had our nine months. I learned to drive and touch-type, then off we went.

First impressions

We passed Dr Powell at sea but Dr Jack Souster was at Ilesha to meet us, and Elsie Ludlow the Matron who had already been there for twenty-five years, and three other Sisters. Jean and I, and our two sons, were shown to the original doctor's bungalow, the one brought from Britain by Dr Stephens, built on stilts, with its wide verandahs on all four sides. We seemed to have front doors north, east, south and west, and it took some getting used to at first! The toilet was a little house perched over a deep pit down the eastern steps. Bucket or pit latrines were still the routine in those days. This was not so different from China, and we soon settled in.

The journey by kit-car from Lagos was by a reasonable tar road all the way and took about six hours. We had come by what was then a new route across the mangrove swamps from Lagos mainland to Ikorudu, and up to Ibadan through Ijebu country, and not through Abeokuta. Ilesha was seventy-five miles north-east of Ibadan the main city of south-west Nigeria, and twenty miles beyond Ile-Ife. There was dense rain-forest beside the rivers, which we crossed carefully by narrow bridges of one car width. Everywhere else there was secondary forest with cocoa plantations, oil palms and farms for maize, yam, cassava and other food crops. Cocoa for chocolate manufacture was the main source of cash for the farmers. The gently hilly country climbed almost imperceptibly to 1200 feet above sea level, giving a slight but welcome cooling to the hot and humid air. Ilesha town's population was about 30,000, a high proportion of them Christian with many churches, and very few mosques. One early duty was to go and pay our respects to the reigning Owa, Oba Haastrup, Ajimoko II, in his bungalow Palace at the centre of the town.

We were pitched straight in to work in hospital and home. Jean learned to grow vegetables and keep hens. No time was given to learn the local language, except for an evening a week, which was insufficient. We never became very fluent. Dr David Cannon arrived in May, and Jack then retired to spend a lot of his time in the hospital office tidying up all the files, correspondence and accounts, and then showing David and me what had to be done to keep things ticking over. David's special interest was in obstetrics and gynaecology, but I was relieved to find that he also enjoyed accounts. We learned our administration the hard way, by having to do it, but fortunately things were relatively simple at that stage.

New disease patterns to learn
Clinical work was very varied. Though much was familiar from my Chinese experience, several conditions - such as yaws and filariasis Loa-loa were new. The kwashiorkor type of malnutrition in children was ubiquitous and tragic, because the mothers had often been trying their best despite poverty and the difficulties of food storage in the hot humid climate. There had been no kwashiorkor in China, perhaps because all babies were breast fed, and had adequate protein through soya bean-curd (tofu) added to their rice-porridge from an early age.

One morning a rather florid-faced British visitor looked in at the morning clinic, saying that he was a doctor interested in children and could he sit and watch. The next patient happened to have kwashiorkor, so I explained its causation in words of one syllable. I asked why he was interested, and to my embarrassment I discovered he was Professor Harold Ellis, author of a well known textbook of paediatrics!

New staff to get to know
Hezekiah Awodiya, the out-patient interpreter, taught the new doctors about the multiple manifestations of yaws ('ogodo' in Yoruba) which produced granulating sores on legs or exposed parts of the body. Acetylarsan was being phased out, and penicillin injections brought in. Even one injection was sufficient. We were also glad to have Hezekiah's assistance in the operating room. It was rumoured that he had done a hernia by himself on one occasion when the doctor was called away.

James Balogun looked after the small laboratory in the OPD, and could do simple blood tests, sputum slides for tuberculosis, skin snips for microfilariae, urine analysis and so on as required. We found his work dependable. Michael Abe produced passable X-ray films - when the machine worked. Mr Laniyan was the mechanic in charge of the generators and Disu Gbadamosi the hospital driver. Somewhat later, Mr S T Popoola (known as Pope) joined the staff as the first true clerical worker, a typist. There was also a cook, a laundryman and a few other labourers and nightwatchmen. Such was our team of men.

Apart from one, the nurses were all women, four missionary sisters, thirteen staff-nurse/midwives, and thirty-five in training. In some extended families the life of girls was fairly tough, and they could be brusque, giving as good as they got. The one male nurse we employed was much gentler. A local newspaper, *The West African Vanguard*, which began publishing in Ilesha, carried articles critical of our girls. I wrote myself to defend them, but it was the town fathers who rose up in support of the nurses who carried the day.

When Dr Souster had tidied up all the office correspondence and accounts, he called David and me in for his hand-over. He initiated us into the book-keeping system, general account and building fund, wages book, and bank statements. He taught us the combination on the lock of the hospital safe and had us check the cash balance together. At the bottom of the safe were some documents which turned out to be the original deeds for the site, three deeds in fact, with land-rent agreements, one at one penny per year, the second at one shilling a year (for an extension of the site in 1928), and the third for the leprosy village land across the road at two shillings per year. It was the first one, dated 1917 and signed by Sir Frederick (later Lord) Lugard, that made us realise our links with the pioneering days of Dr Stephens and the heritage we were taking on.

Jack and Marian Souster, and their two daughters, travelled home at the end of July. They had done so much to help our family find their feet. David and I had the responsibility for the hospital on our shoulders, but with Elsie's mature advice to fall back on. Fortunately David proved an excellent colleague, with a delightful sense of humour and a deep commitment. We enjoyed ten years together and I could not have had a better partner on the job. Dr John Wright FRCS joined us in 1953, and for the first time in its history the hospital had the luxury of three doctors, allowing a minimum of two when one was away on leave. Mr Ken Parker, an engineer friend of David's, came to help with the rebuilding.

Supervising the rebuilding of the hospital

Developing architect's skills

Neither David nor I had any previous experience of building. Jack had shown us the copies of plans prepared by John Powell, covering out-patient department, welfare, wards, offices and nurses homes. They were simple ground plans, with little or no detail or specifications, and interpretation was in the hands of Mr Jobling the builder. He had undertaken to complete everything at a rate of one shilling and sixpence per cubic-foot, and that was that. There was no formal contract document. Harry, and his wife Nellie, were a bluff Yorkshire pair who got things done, and no nonsense, when they were there. Nellie kept watch on site and made sure that enough cement went in with the sand. Whenever out-doors she wore a double felt hat to keep off the sun. Harry and his foreman, Badamosi, supervised the carpenters, and the quality of work in the mahogany roof trusses and window frames could not have been bettered. Unfortunately the Joblings had other projects in hand, including a memorial church in Badagry on the coast, so the doctors had to sort out problems in between visits. Plans for the Operating Theatre and Maternity Department had to be re-drawn, but within the limitations of the original dimensions. At one point Harry asked about the staff houses which John Powell had not had time to draw, though it was agreed that five should be included. This was a challenge. Missionaries of the past had tended to build large houses for themselves, and smaller ones for their national colleagues. It had been the same in China. It was resolved to build sensible-sized houses acceptable to expatriates or Nigerian staff. If anything, we made the houses too small, but they proved adequate.

A major decision was whether the time had come for the mini-revolution of changing from pit and bucket latrines to water-borne sanitation. The change could triple water requirements. Adequate water from a stream which ran along one perimeter of the new site, and pumped to a high-level tank, was in the plans, and it was judged that W.C's and septic tanks would be practicable. However there was nothing in the plans, and no experienced person to guide us. Any information was avidly sought after, and I spent so much time reading up the technology my colleagues said they would award me the 'D.D.' - 'Doctor of drains'! In the event, all was well.

In March 1953 the first doctor's house on the new site was completed, and David and Ken moved in, so as to assist with supervision there. Work was completed a year later, and it was only then, as the profit for Blaize was being worked out, that we realised the drawback of having no written form of contract. There was some acrimony which had to be sorted out with a further deferred payment agreement. It was a lesson I was to learn for the future. Even with the best of friends, where money is concerned, it is better to have everything written down and signed for.

Fig 3.1 *Dr Pearson, Dr Cannon and Ken Parker in front of the Sisters' House on the old site*

Fig 3.2 *Michael, Dr Pearson's eldest son, with a toy engine left behind by a previous family, in front of the original Stephens bungalow where the Pearsons first lived*

Vital help from an engineer

Later this year we received help from Mr John Mellanby, a highly-qualified free-lance engineer, brother of the Professor Kenneth Mellanby, the first Vice-chancellor of the University at Ibadan. Having overseen the electrical installation there in the 1940s, he had helped John Powell with improving the infrastructure at the old hospital. Now he came to help at the new, putting in the pair of 10 kva generators for the engine-house, and the overhead distribution system round the compound. He also installed a vertical wood-burning boiler, to produce low pressure steam for sterilising in the theatre and maternity departments, a clean and cost-effective system. John's help and advice was always useful, and there was no area of engineering, electrical, mechanical, ventilation or sanitary, to which he could not turn his hand. One thing he proposed was a central sewage system for the entire compound, with recovery of water from the effluent, and re-circulation after sedimentation for low-risk use like sluicing toilets. On this occasion we turned him down, thinking local opinion would not be ready to accept such a radical suggestion. In view of the subsequent dire water shortage, we may have been wrong.

Moving begins

In March 1954 the Pearsons moved house, then other staff as residences were made ready. In April the old hospital wards were gradually emptied, then finally closed to in-patients for six weeks. Out-patients only ceased for four days. All visitors and friends who came anywhere near the hospital at that time found themselves conscripted into the work of transferring all the hospital furniture, equipment, drugs and linen. We had very little extra money at this stage. New beds were in hand but all bedside tables, and many other items of furniture, were made by our own team of carpenters from local hardwoods. Joseph Erimuhai, the head carpenter, was to stay on with the hospital till his retirement; he did such beautiful work. A heavy responsibility rested on Elsie Ludlow as the Matron with all her knowledge of what was needed.

Water

At one point the hospital was offered a bulldozer which had broken down in the bush - if we could mend it. Ken Parker did, and put it to work levelling the site where it was necessary. He also supervised the construction of the 10,000 gallon overhead water tank which was to be the hospital's source of gravity feed and reserve supply. We were wor-

Fig 3.3 *Harry and Nellie Jobling, builders of the new hospital, using the first office building for a temporary home*

Fig 3.4 *View from the Male Ward to the Children's ward before the covered way was built*

ried. The water from the stream was looking increasingly unlikely to meet the hospital's needs. Then in June the first mains water to the town, from a dam in the mountains of Effon Alaiye twenty miles away, was completed and turned on. The hospital was connected but no-one really knew if the pressure would be sufficient to reach the hospital which was on relatively high ground. One day, the water began to flow, and we held our breath. I connected up a hose-pipe, climbed with it up the steps to the top of the high tank, and the water did not cease to flow till the pipe was ten feet above that! How cheered we were! The water was unpurified at that time, and often quite brown from river silt, but at least it was plentiful. By filtration and boiling it could be made safe. The first operations in the new theatre (though with its old name 'Ream Memorial Theatre (RMT)' retained) took place soon after. If only that pressure of water had been sustained through the years to come. The pace of development of Ilesha town, and the vastly increased water demand as everyone switched to water-borne sanitation proved too much, and a chronic shortage began - but that is another stage in the story.

Drug supplies

David Cannon returned from leave in July 1954 having married one of our nursing sisters, Margaret Ingham. She continued to work with the nursing team, but, in addition, having been given a 'Missionary Permit to Dispense' by the government, she looked after the pharmacy. It was to be another six years before we could afford and recruit a fully qualified pharmacist (Miss K Owen). The doctors took responsibility for the drug store, and for ordering fresh supplies. There was already quite a range of effective drugs, sulphonamides, penicillin, dapsone, tetracycline etc but full use was also made of the ingredients which went into the common Mixtures - Mist.Alba, Mist.Expect, Mist.Stramonium et Pot.Iod., and so on.

Landscaping the new compound

The story of WGH Ilesha is not complete without mention of the invaluable help given by the missionary wives. As Margaret Cannon helped with dispensing, my wife, Jean, helped with the hospital grounds. All the land covered with buildings had been cleared completely, with the exception of the palm trees that were harvested by a palm-oil maker, and some large trees and a magnificent grove of bamboos along the stream on the southern border of the site. Jean enjoyed naming the roads, Nim Avenue, Flamboyant Road and Frangipani Drive, and plant-

Fig 3.5 *Joseph the carpenter, who began making hospital furniture on the old site, and continued as head carpenter in the new hospital*

Fig 3.6 *Dr Pearson beside the notice-board at the entrance to the new site, with out-patient buildings behind*

ing the appropriate trees, though usually on one side rather than both, because of the overhead electric distribution wires. Around the wards, and the covered ways between them, low ice-plant hedges were placed to stop erosion by rain from the roofs. The grass was kept cut neatly by men using petrol or electric motor-mowers. Eman Fakuade was to become head gardener under her guidance, and the hospital grounds were always kept colourful and tidy, an important contribution to the hospital appearance atmosphere. Beauty can be therapeutic. Other missionary wives contributed freely from their variety of skills.

Looking forwards
Dr Joyce and the Rev. Nelson Ludlow were still in the country, but working mainly in the northern region at Afon, Ilorin and further north along the River Niger at Kaiama and Bussa. They still carried on their mobile work, combining health promotion and evangelism. When pioneering around Afon in 1936 they had made use of an Austin Seven car which they had bought in Ilesha for £25. It proved ideal for going down the bush-paths through the grasslands. After the war they acquired a bigger and better mobile unit van, but when I first visited Afon in 1952 the 'baby Austin' tourer was still in its shed there, looking rather like an overgrown pram! Before retiring that year the Ludlows called at Ilesha WGH and gave some useful advice.

> 'If ever the government asks the hospital to give free treatment in return for a grant-in-aid, be sure that you ask for a per-capita payment for each patient who attends. Do not accept a fixed sum per year'

Her advice was to prove very wise not so long after.

When the entire nursing staff moved over to the new site, we realised how ad-hoc had been our arrangements. Elsie Ludlow pointed out that the nurses had to eat, and there was no dining hall. At the old hospital it had been convenient for them to use a wide section of verandah at the end of the Male Ward, close to the hospital kitchen. There was no such place in the new hospital. As a temporary solution the hospital lorry and kit-car were moved out of the garage provided, and the nurses dining tables put up in there.

One of the last buildings to go up was the hospital gate-house. This was deliberately made to look like the old hospital gate-house, though with

Fig 3.7 *Mr John Mellanby, free-lance engineer, who gave such invaluable help*

a wider, higher entrance to accommodate larger vehicles coming in. Across the arch was the name 'WESLEY GUILD HOSPITAL', and above it space for the carved Guild badge, two feet diameter, painted blue and gold, a gift sent out by the Guild Holiday Homes in Britain.

Placing the badge in position was left to be part of the Official Opening ceremony of the hospital on September 25th 1954. This was a great occasion, preceded by a march through the town from the old hospital to the new. At the old, the name sign was taken down, and prayers were offered from a loud-speaker van, and the procession set off headed by the nurses carrying the Guild badge, and followed by other hospital staff, scouts, guides and contingents from every church and every school in town, with sundry noisy bands. Dr Powell, who had been invited back from England for the occasion, marched and danced with them. At the new hospital gate there was a platform for the Owa and chiefs, and other guests from church and State, and a crowd of 3000 well-wishers. After the speeches and messages of good-will from Nigeria and Britain, I climbed a near vertical ladder to place the Guild Badge in its slot above the gatehouse arch. The Minister of Health, Mr Ighodaro, performed the opening ceremony and the crowds swarmed through the gates to inspect every corner of the new hospital. Another £1000 was collected in donations from those who formally opened the many doors.

Thankfulness to have the move complete

The hospital was deeply indebted to all those who helped to make the rebuilding possible, both from within Nigeria and from overseas. The appeal for £2500 from young Methodists and Guilders in Britain had captured their imagination throughout the country, and thanks were given to them at the opening ceremony. In addition we put up a plaque at the entrance to the hospital wards to remind us of the ethos of the Methodist Youth Department at the time:

> *We gratefully remember the members of Wesley Guilds and Methodist Youth Clubs in the United Kingdom, who collected over £2500 towards the rebuilding of this hospital.*

Methodist Youth Charter

In life — *devoted*
In church — *a family*
In person — *fit*
In faith — *equipped*
In service — *world citizens.*

The move had been made just in time to allow the hospital to make the most of new opportunities which were about to open up.

CHAPTER 4

NEW OPPORTUNITIES, 1955–1959

The last days of colonialism

When we arrived in Nigeria in 1952 it was a British colony, and many of the old colonial attitudes and prejudices remained. Reluctance to pass on real responsibility was common among the Europeans who assumed they were the only ones who could take charge. Africans should keep their place. After my experience of China, post revolution, I found this difficult to accept, but it was true even in the hospital. When a deputation of junior nurses came to ask for more pay the reaction was one of horror at their very impudence! We had a small staff Advisory Committee but it consisted of the missionaries alone. There was no Nigerian representation. The situation was about to change.

The process of transforming the British Empire into the Commonwealth had begun. In 1955 the British Government started preparing Nigeria for independence. Regional autonomy was granted to the Western Region and Eastern Region in the southern half of Nigeria, but not to the Northern Region which was not considered ready. East and West elected their own Assemblies with certain powers, which included Health. Ilesha was in the Western Region, and its first elected Premier was Chief Obafemi Awolowo, a personable, clear-thinking lawyer, with a real concern for his country and good 'social skills'. We had met him on the boat travelling home for our first leave. He had left his First Class companions and came to the Cabin Class passengers to organize and play in a draughts tournament. He was quick to make friends - and he won the tournament! He was leader of the Action Party which had campaigned for a free health service for children under the age of eighteen years, on the assumption that if the country was not wealthy enough to provide a national health service for everyone, the younger generation should have priority.

Start of the free health service for children

Once in power he put his programme into action, assisted by an efficient civil service, which was one sound legacy of the colonial days. The government health facilities ceased to charge even the token fees formerly levied on children. Awolowo knew that up to half the health service in his Region was given by the mission hospitals, so these were then approached to see if they could join his scheme. From Ilesha we replied (remembering Dr Ludlow's advice) that we could do so if a grant based on per-capita attendance could be paid each quarter. The Director of Medical Services sent a letter agreeing, and offering one shilling per out-patient attendance. We replied and said that one shilling was too little, but three would do; a sum was also suggested for each inpatient admission. The other mission hospitals in the Region came along with us. The DMS accepted our proposals, and by April 1955 the Free Treatment for Under 18's scheme was in operation, and was to last for ten years. Three letters, and the deal was done! Never again were negotiations with government so simple.

What a relief it was to be able to offer all the children who attended whatever treatment they needed, without having to recover the cost from their parents. There was no system of birth certification, and ages often had to be assessed in relation to historical landmarks such as the month the hospital moved, or a new Owa was enthroned. With the school-children it was surprising how long they remained seventeen! We learned to look at teeth, and if all four wisdom teeth were through they were deemed to be eighteen. If we erred it was on the generous side.

It was not common at that time for hospitals even to have a paediatric ward. Children shared space, usually in the women's ward. The news that Ilesha had a dedicated children's ward in which treatment was free, apart from a charge made for feeding, spread through the town and well beyond. Children with the most severe kwashiorkor, post-measles bronchopneumonia, whooping cough, tuberculosis or cancrum-oris, came to us, sometimes as their last hope. The new hospital had four main wards, male, female, maternity and children's, plus a small isolation ward; and three doctors, though often only two because one would be on leave. We shared the work between us, and it was heavy. We all had to be generalists. At the beginning of 1955 it fell to John Wright to look after the children's ward, though he was, in fact, by speciality, a surgeon, and a thoracic surgeon at that! He was appalled that despite all the energetic treatment given on the ward there was still a death rate of up to one in four of those admitted. The children were just coming too late. They often suffered from multiple pathology, such as post-measles kwashiorkor with pneumonia and diarrhoea. Sometimes therapy worked, but all too often the children just faded away, and the agonized wailing of the mothers was heard throughout the hospital, sometimes several in a day.

Proposal for child health research

Dr Wright then made the brilliantly wild suggestion to Dr Cannon and myself that we cut back our work in the hospital, and spend half our time in the villages outside, treating these children at an earlier stage when they could still be saved! Logical, but how to do it? We agreed with him in theory, but were well aware it would be next to impossible to reduce our hospital work-load, given present staffing. Maybe, if we had another doctor ....? John said he would get in touch with someone involved with Dr Donald Court and his Thousand Family longitudinal research project on the health of children in Newcastle. This was our introduction to Dr David Morley, paediatrician. In the ensuing correspondence it was proposed that, to solve our problem properly, a community-based research programme was needed in Nigeria to find out what were the commonest illnesses from which the children were dying, and what methods could best prevent this mortality. David agreed to come and do this study if we could get the funding. A first approach was made to the West African Council of Medical Research in Lagos, headed by Colonel Dr John Walters. He had his doubts. Laboratory-based research was their style.

At about this time a visiting doctor from the World Health Organization called at Ilesha, and asked what were our main concerns. We talked about the child health dilemma, and she sympathised. A few days later, when given an opportunity to put our case to Dr Walters at his WACMR headquarters in Yaba, Lagos, I had to wait outside his office while he finished with someone else. When this person came out it turned out to be the WHO doctor! It appeared that she had prepared the way so well that when it came to my turn to put our request, Dr Walters agreed at once. He could not provide one of WACMR's usual grants, but he would provide a 'subvention' for a five-year longitudinal study under Wesley Guild Hospital control, subject only to submitting our reports to WACMR. It was unusual for mission hospitals to be involved in research, and the first time for WGH, but what an important decision that was to be. David Morley, an Anglican whom the Church Missionary Society had been unable to accept because they had no specialist post, happily agreed to come to WGH Ilesha as a Methodist missionary. That was in 1956.

Nigerianization begins in earnest

The hospital was moving in other ways too. Nigerian staff were promoted and allowed to carry responsibility. Mr Hezekiah Awodiya was made Assistant Hospital Manager. Mrs Rebecca Komolafe was made Assistant Nursing Sister, and full Sister in 1962. The Methodist Church, Nigeria, accepted a new Constitution for the hospital, passing much of the executive control to a Hospital Management Committee (HMC) with local church, community and government representatives. The wording of the Constitution was based on one produced by the Voluntary Health Association of India, with modifications to suit our need. The Methodist Superintendent of the Circuit was made the Chairman, and among the church representatives two laymen from Otapete Methodist Church, Mr D D Layinka, and Mr J O Ogunseitan, were to give outstanding service for many years. For the first time the Ilesha community felt they had an effective voice in the hospital's affairs. The HMC proved a very successful governing body, and undertook a host of new developments. For day to day affairs within the hospital the constitution specified a monthly Staff Committee comprising the main hospital officers, and representatives from the nurses and the workers. It provided transparency and also worked well.

No escape from more building

When we moved up to the new hospital site, all of us fondly hoped we had done with building, though we knew there was a Nurses Dining Hall to produce sometime. Early in 1955 Elsie Ludlow came up with a proposal which she said was even more urgent. We needed a Hospital Chapel, one where the staff and nursing students could have morning and evening prayers. She suggested it be built in memory of Sister Stella Liony, the pioneer of nurse training, who had died in 1953. This was agreed, and a Methodist architect friend of mine in Britain, Mr Brian Searle, produced the design, which was approved at the first HMC in June 1955. A local Methodist builder, Mr J O Martin, agreed to put it up for £2000, building the wall of block stone, the light brown granite from Mount Imo quarry north of Ilesha town. One feature was a belltower separate from the main structure, and the Guilds in Britain agreed to donate the bell. Joseph, carpenter, made all the pews to the highest of standards using local iroko timber. All was ready for opening by April 1956, which happened to be the day after which David Morley and his family arrived.

Another building came as a surprise. One day a patient in the Isolation Ward, Mr J O Layide, stopped me on my rounds. He had been extremely ill, but was recovering.

Doctor' he said, 'I have got two requests. One, give me the best injection you have got to complete my cure, even if it costs £5. Two, I want to build a new Private Ward Block for the hospital with five rooms'. When we had recovered from our incredulity, he went on to explain that he was a plank dealer with some money saved up, and wanted to spend it on something of permanent value before he died. 'God has sent me to you' he said. The offer was accepted, plans drawn up and approved by him and the HMC and work begun. However, Mr Layide's impulsive generosity was to prove an embarrassment. His savings ran out, building stopped half way, and it was two years before completion - with hospital help.

In 1956 the HMC approved rebuilding of the Leprosy Village on a 22-acre site in the country a mile north of the hospital. The Local Council leased the land, granted £900, and the Colonial Development and Welfare Fund granted £3,500 on the recommendation of the Divisional Officer, Mr K.Y.M. MacKenzie. A ring of houses was built, and also a small chapel financed from the Rank Trust. Many of the patients at the village near the old hospital were actively rehabilitated, and discharged to their communities. The new village was opened with the remaining six patients, plus fresh admissions from among those presenting at the hospital out-patient department, and needing active care with the curative drugs available. The name 'leper' was forbidden. These were leprosy patients, on a par with sufferers from any other disease. One week-end when I was at home, but on duty for emergencies, I received a call from a boy who had brought his father, who he said had been ill for a year. He did not know what it was. I demurred. This was no emergency. I said, 'Call back on Monday'. He went away, but came again to say, 'Please come now'. His father was afraid to come back on Monday. Very odd. So, I went, and as soon as I saw the father I understood. He was suffering from the kind of lepromatous leprosy that gives a 'leonine facies', a face like a lion, and a fearsome, pathetic sight he was. He had spent a year in the bush, afraid to show himself to anyone, but the son had heard of WGH Ilesha and brought him. I congratulated the boy for disturbing my week-end rest. The father was admitted to the new village, treated with dapsone, and eventually he made a full recovery, with face, ears and limbs restored so well you would hardly have believed he had ever had leprosy. Other cases followed, and the village was soon full, but with an active turnover as those who were cured went home. While in residence they used the land around to farm. Some wove rush baskets. It was always a joy to go and lead prayers there on a Sunday.

The opening of the Stella Liony Memorial Chapel on April 7th 1956 was a rather special day. It was the first function performed by the Rev. Daniel B Esan after coming to Ilesha as Superintendent of the Circuit. He was said to have had some link with Dr Stephens when he was a boy in Igbo-Ora in 1912, but in any case he became a close friend of the hospital, Chairman of the HMC and a valued adviser and supporter through thick and thin. And what a voice he had! He once hailed me across the busy hubbub of the traffic outside Kingsway in Lagos, and the voice carried clearly, and quite unmistakably! The Rev. Alan Angus, the District Chairman, was there, and a representative of the Shagamu Wesley Guild who pulled the bell-rope to give the first peal on the Guild bell! David and Aileen Morley and family arrived just in time for the day.

From 1956 the practice began of issuing an illustrated Hospital Report giving essential statistics of hospital activities, names of current staff, and details of new developments. It was felt that the local community, and all supporters of the hospital, should know what was happening. The first report was welcomed, and it was produced every other year subsequently until 1974/75.

In 1958 the Electricity Corporation of Nigeria (ECN) brought mains power to Ilesha, and the hospital was connected up. The generators could now be kept for emergencies when mains power failed. The Posts and Telegraphs Department (P & T) installed telephone connections to all buildings in the hospital, and a small, manually operated internal exchange for twenty-five lines (later fifty). This seemingly minor development brought enormous advantages. Previously there had been just the one line to the hospital, and the one telephone which was situated

Fig 4.1 *The rebuilt leprosy village*

Fig 4.2 *Morning queue for the Under Fives Clinic*

at the end of the verandah of the Medical Superintendent's house. It was generally Mrs Pearson who had to be the hospital telephonist and either take messages, or send for the doctor or other person required. Now, though we still had only one external line, we had extensions in all the main wards and departments of the hospital, and all the staff houses on site. Internal or external (or even overseas) calls could be made from any outlet. The telephone operator worked at his 'PBX' in the Admission Room at the main entrance to the wards, and also covered other clerical duties for the patients. One clerk worked through the night, and what a boon that was for night calls! Previously, when a doctor was required in the small hours, a night watchman or ward maid was sent to tap on the doctor's bedroom window and give the message, 'Dokita, please come'. The uneducated messenger was quite unable to answer enquiries about the nature of the emergency, except to say it was in the maternity, or children's ward or wherever, and frustrations were many! With the new system, the night sister could get through to the doctor on duty direct, describe the case and often obtain permission to manage the case herself according to doctor's advice. If the doctor had to be there, for a Caesarean section, say, he could give preliminary instructions, and find things ready in the operating theatre when he arrived. What a relief that was! Conserving time for sleep was important. Normal duty began next morning at 7.00 or 8.00am irrespective of night time interruptions.

The Morley revolution

David Morley's coming was to present us with opportunities and challenges which changed the direction of the hospital. The WACMR subvention covered half David's costs, and the MMS covered the other half, so it was agreed his time should be divided, half for research and the other half for clinical work. His research time was 'protected'. As a paediatrician he was put in charge of seeing children, but given time to analyse his records so that he could work out, for instance, the ten commonest causes of illness and death, and the ways we could apply means of prevention or early treatment, so as to prevent the rapid descent into life-threatening illness.

In the children's ward he worked with our first Nigerian nursing sister, Mrs Rebecca Komolafe, and introduced the concept that the mother's place was beside her child. No longer would mothers be sent home, and only admitted for Visiting Hours. They would stay, except for an hour morning and evening when the ward was being cleaned, and this included staying over night. They would bring a sleeping mat to unroll to sleep there beside the cot. What a relief! The children were so much happier. A Mothers' Shelter was built close to the ward, where the mothers could keep their loads, have a shower, wash their clothes or just rest while the ward was being cleaned. The old regime, where the mothers were chased away from the ward at night, for instance, had been wrong, but it was one imported from Britain. Now it has changed there too. The danger of maternal deprivation has been recognized. Even in the tropics, children alone in a cot can get cold, and at night when very ill can even die from hypothermia. Under this new regime, the doctor on his night round would sometimes find the cot empty and the child on the floor with mother, warm and comfortable and happy. We learned not to object. Touch and maternal warmth are more important than a tidy ward. The African mother obviously knew that by instinct.

The Imesi-Ile research scheme begins

In October 1956 Sister Margaret Woodland arrived to work with David, as part of his WACMR team. Health-visitor trained, and with previous overseas experience in Sarawak, she was well suited to the community-based research programme on which she and David now embarked. Imesi-Ile village, twenty-five miles away was chosen, and a two-storey Nigerian-style house in the village adapted for her to live in. Mrs Mary Bifarin was the nurse-midwife in charge of the Methodist dispensary/maternity home, first established in the days of Joyce Ludlow. A survey of all the houses and families in the village of 5000 people was first done, so as to get base-line figures and profile of the population. It was found that 450 out of every 1000 children born were dying by the age of five years, and this was probably average for the area. A new records system was started, and growth charts were introduced for all the Under Fives. From the 1st January 1957 every baby born was enrolled in the research scheme, and a red star put on their chart. As David records in his book (1),

> 'Over the next eighteen months, 413 children were born into the village, and 404 of these were included in our study and closely followed up at least monthly ... over five years. This longitudinal study was the first of its size to be undertaken in Tropical Africa'.

The nine births not included were to families in a pentecostal Christian group which did not believe in medicines, and therefore would not come to the dispensary. Nevertheless Sister Woodland and her staff knew about them. When the drumming started in the village to announce a birth a midwife went directly to the house to give her congratulations, offer advice and collect the information for her records. Likewise, if there were deaths in the village, or any calamity, the health workers were there, going out of their way to help, night or day. It was the caring spirit of these dedicated Christian workers which ensured the close cooperation of the entire community throughout the years of the study, and made it so unique and valuable.

David was an 'active research' person, not one for pigeon-holing his findings. As he developed ideas he came to me as Medical Superintendent for the means to put them to work. His proposals were always so sensible, simple and economical, they could easily be implemented. True, he came to Ilesha at an opportune time. The Free Treatment scheme was in effect, both for the hospital and for its out-stations, including Imesi-Ile. As more patients were attracted by his approach, the more returns we sent to government, and the greater our per-capita grant. The grant for in-patients was too low, but the three shillings per out-patient was a little high, and made up for the losses on in-patients. David's successful methods were therefore self-financing.

A new style of health care at WGH Ilesha

The preliminary studies had shown that 90% of the child deaths were occurring in the first five years. The first year was hazardous, as had long been known, but the second and third years were as bad, as the children met the dangers of malnutrition, malaria, measles, whooping cough, diarrhoea, pneumonia and so much else. The infant welfare department at the hospital was therefore re-designed to cope with all children up to the age of five years. Large waiting spaces were added in front of the clinic to accommodate the growing numbers of patients. David noticed that the usual 18-inch (45cm) high bench was uncomfortable for toddler mums, because it made their laps slope away. 14-inch (35cm) benches gave them a level lap on which it was so much easier to sit their children. All benches were therefore cut to fourteen inches.

The weight-chart David used for Imesi was used at base hospital too. It had space to graph the child's weight-for-age over the first five years.

The drug firm, Glaxo, funded it, in association with a high-protein child weaning food, 'Amama', made from groundnuts, which they were then promoting. Growth curves showing the average weights of healthy children, based on local findings, were drawn on the graph. Previous research workers had used weight-for-age graphs with a vertical line to denote each month. David's innovation was to allow an 8mm-wide column for each month, and in this the month of birth and each succeeding month could be written in by hand along the bottom. It was a very simple change, but by it the graph was transformed from a research tool into a clinical tool, and a practical aid to health monitoring. Other events in the child's life like the starting of solid food, or an attack of diarrhoea or measles, could also be written into the appropriate column as they occurred. The chart now recorded not just the weight-for-age, but important nutritional factors and illnesses causing weight loss or gain along the way. Upper and lower lines on the graph showed the average weight to aim at, and a lower limit below which was danger. Serious deviation from the normal was thus made immediately visible, often before the mother even realised something was wrong. The 'Amama Card' was the prototype for the growth charts based on internationally accepted figures now used world-wide.

David also introduced the practice of allowing the mother to keep the child's record at home, supplying her with an appropriate-sized polythene bag in which to keep the cards clean and dry. She was taught to bring the record with her on every attendance, whether for the routine monthly welfare visit, or in emergencies. People were astonished to find how well the cards were cared for, and brought on every occasion. No longer did cards have to be filed, and retrieved at each visit with the expenditure of much time and labour. It was soon shown that the loss rate by the mothers was less than that due to mis-filing of records stored in the hospital. What were to become known as 'home-based records' had come to stay.

The next step was to arrange for Grade II midwives and nurses to see the mothers and their children before they were taken to a doctor. In doing this David was, without realising it, able to build on foundations already laid by the Ludlows. Two of his most effective midwives were ones who had worked with Joyce Ludlow in the clinics at Afon and Kaiama in Ilorin Circuit, Wende Awoseye and Victoria Thompson. They in turn helped others. David gave them written 'Guidance Notes' as to how to interpret the weight chart, advise the mother on immunisations, and look for minor treatable illness. By following these their skills increased, and they were soon able to cope with up to 90% of the under fives. They knew which serious cases must be referred to a doctor. The first *Under Fives Welfare Clinic* evolved before our eyes, and proved popular with the mothers. Patient-attendances began to climb. By 1958, total out-patients had doubled from 76,000 before David began his changes, to 144,000, of which 103,000 (72%) were under eighteen. By 1960 the total was 200,000 of which 160,000 (80%) were under eighteen. Mothers would start queuing at 5.00 am ready for registration at 7.00 am. It was a common sight to see an orderly row of buckets, bags and bundles stretching from the clinic door for a hundred metres out to the main gate, as the mothers marked their place in the queue while they went out to the food vendors to get some breakfast, or to find a quiet spot to feed their children!

When the Welfare doors opened, the person who first met the patients was Matthew Agboh, who, with two assistants sat at the desk registering hospital number, and weighing each child and putting the dot on the graph. Very ill children would be picked out of the queue by a staff-nurse and brought to the front for immediate attention. Others sat down for a health talk, before seeing their community midwife, receiving advice on nutrition, getting an immunisation or medicine. Just one in ten had to go to the doctor's consulting room for further check-up. All would be seen, and on their way home by 1.00 pm.

Matthew was a gem. He had first come to WGH with a serious injury to his right arm, requiring amputation. He had been travelling from his home village 300 miles away in search of employment. His hopes of finding work were dashed and the outlook grim. While in hospital, however, he learned to write with his left hand, and became so adept he was made registration clerk for the Under Fives Clinic. Though not a local man no person could have done it better. Surrounded by a crowd of 500 anxious mothers and their babies and toddlers, some very sick, he could keep his cool, work steadily and efficiently, and never raise his voice. His word and a smile must have reassured so many. He continued on that job till retirement thirty-five years later. He had a firm and simple faith. In a Christian meeting he even thanked God that the loss of his arm had led to the opportunity for such service in the hospital.

Other changes introduced by Dr Morley

Although the paediatric work and Imesi-Ile research took most of David's energy he still found time to help at the Ilesha hospital in a variety of other ways. He worked with John Wright in establishing a clinic for tuberculosis cases, which were all too common, recognizing that the disease could be better treated if all cases, once diagnosed, came at a particular time each week, and were given a special card to ensure consistent regular care. The Tuberculosis Clinic ultimately became my special interest, with an unexpected research outcome.

The Imesi programme required more routine laboratory investigations than our one technician working in a small room in the out-patient department at Ilesha could cope with. It was David who pushed the hospital to build a larger central laboratory, with more staff, and with equipment provided from his WACMR research fund. This extended in 1958 to developing the hospital's first blood bank which was to save so many lives, such as adults with severe injuries and children with acute malarial anaemia. One cultural problem was encountered when trying to recruit voluntary donors. Some people feared that if their blood was given to a stranger, that person would then have power over them. When Christian members of staff gave blood and showed there was nothing to fear, others happily followed. The transfusion service took off. In the maternity department it helped cut mortality of mothers from nineteen in 1957 (897 deliveries), down to five in 1958 (954 deliveries).

Through the link with WACMR a mobile virus research laboratory from Lagos was stationed at the hospital for some months. It was a caravan full of white mice in little cages - and one scientist. Serum from every child with a probable virus fever was injected into a mouse, and any mouse which succumbed was examined to see what virus was responsible. About six viruses were found, and among them was a new strain of arbovirus which had never been isolated before. It therefore rejoices in the name *Ilesha Virus,* and is in all the scientific text-books, but apart from knowing that it gave one child a fever it has not yet been related to any more serious disease syndrome.

Surgery, and other departments

Dr Wright left at the end of 1956, and through 1957 Dr Cannon and I had to share the surgery. Dr Roy Goonewardene from Sri Lanka arrived in 1958, with his English wife, Beryl. Roy was supported by the Methodist

Church in Sri Lanka as 'their missionary', and the Wesley Guild in Colombo made a financial contribution. Surgery was his interest, and after one year he went to Britain and gained his FRCS qualification, both in London and Edinburgh. After returning, he developed the method of providing day surgery for hernia cases, a technique now becoming widely used around the world. While in Ilesha Roy completed his training as a Methodist Local Preacher, did his 'trial sermon' at the Otapete Church in the town. He survived a grilling by the Local Preachers' Committee and was accepted onto Full Plan. He grew a bushy black beard and looked like an Old Testament prophet, and he sounded like one when he led prayers in the hospital chapel. When he was teaching surgery to nurses, he brooked no interruptions. Anyone caught talking was peremptorily ordered out. At a Christmas party the nurses got their own back by performing a skit on the nursing school. The girls were all so good at acting. When Eunice Fakande came in as 'Dr Roy' to start her lecture before the assembled students she had everyone in stitches as one student after another was directed with out-stretched arm towards the door as she declaimed imperiously, 'Out! Out! Out!' - till the classroom was deserted!

In 1958 Enid Blake completed ten years as the first Sister Tutor and left in April. No qualified successor was found for over two years, but Sister Marion Lethbridge took on the work, as Acting Tutor, and the School continued to do well. Later that year the Nurses' Dining Hall was completed - a fine group of buildings which included the kitchen, a reception room where nurses could meet their families and boy-friends, and a residence for the Nurses Home Warden. Brian Searle was the architect, and the warm brown block stone from Mount Imo was used again to good effect.

Ante-natal clinics for expectant mothers were initially held in the same building as the Child Welfare. As the paediatric work continued to grow, in 1959 a new Ante-natal block was built close by with an excellently functional design. The welfare space vacated was used mainly for the school children who made much use of the free-treatment system. They too were dealt with mainly by a staff-nurse, just the few with more serious problems, or those requiring surgery, being sent to a doctor.

University link-up

Dr Morley's style of child health work attracted visitors from the medical

Fig 4.3 *Sister Enid Blake, first qualified Sister Tutor, at her send-off in April 1958*

Back row:
Mr Balogun,
Dr Morley,
Dr Pearson,
Dr Goonewardene,
Dr Cannon,
Pastor Oshinguwa

Middle row:
Mr Popooola,
Mrs Awoseye,
Mrs Silva,
Mr Awodiya,
Mr Abe,
Mrs Thompson

Front row:
Miss Grant,
Mrs Komolafe,
Miss Ludlow,
Miss Lethbridge,
Miss Rowding

Fig 4.4 Senior Staff in 1958

school at Ibadan, seventy-five miles away, beginning with Professor Bob Collis and followed later by Professor Ralph Hendrickse of the U.C.H. Paediatric Department. In 1959, David was invited to be a Part-time Lecturer by the university, and Ilesha was asked to receive six or seven medical students for a week's posting during their senior year of child health training. We housed them in the Private Block, and allowed them to feed with the nurses. Bob Collis persuaded the drug company, Glaxo-Allenburys, to offer a grant of £6000 to build a Students' Hostel, but the hospital had some hesitation in accepting. We knew Dr Morley was due to complete his time in 1961, and had no idea whether anyone with similar skills and vision would succeed him. Neither was it clear that a mission hospital should have a permanent commitment to teaching medical students. Glaxo reassured us there were no strings attached. 'Use the buildings as you wish' they said; so the offer was gladly accepted. Again, Brian Searle did the designing, and a most useful and attractive complex consisting of rooms for students and junior doctors, with a communal dining hall and kitchen, was to be the result. The Hostel cemented the university link, and this was to be more important than we could possibly have realised. The postings of Ibadan medical students became a permanent feature, and, though none could have forseen it then, WGH was ultimately, in 1975, to become part of a teaching hospital - but under another medical school.

CHAPTER 5

MUCH TO CELEBRATE, 1960–1969

Independence for Nigeria

1960 was the year that Nigeria achieved its independence from the British Empire. The Federal Republic of Nigeria was born, and on October 1st the Union Jack was lowered and the new white and green striped flag raised over the Northern Region, as well as in Western and Eastern Regions which had received limited autonomy five years before. The first elected Governor-General was Dr Nnamide Azikwe, the Eastern Region leader, and a Northern teacher, Tafewa Balewa, was made the Prime Minister, receiving widespread respect. Chief Awolowo became Leader of the Opposition. This regionalisation of politics, east plus north against west, was not to bode well for a secure future, though everyone hoped for the best. As evidence that fears were not fully allayed, within two years Awolowo was even put on trial for treason!

The euphoria of October 1st, Independence Day, was made the most of in Lagos, with street decorations from London's Regent Street, and a fleet of 'Independence cars' in green and white stripes to ferry VIP's around. Up country, we did things our own way. The hospital sisters and nurses all bought lengths of 'Independence cloth' covered with a design of Nigeria maps and flags in the regulation green and white. We had a watch-night service the evening before, and the nurses partied until 1.00 am. Chiefs from the town brought presents for the first baby born on the day. There were group photographs and a communal meal for all hospital staff, and plenty of dancing. We were particularly pleased that among the government-invited guests were Dr Hunter, Chief Olu-Awo of Ilesha, and his wife Doris. In Ilesha they were given a great family welcome by hospital, church and town. Dr Morley and Margaret Woodland organized a Medical Exhibition in the town-hall to depict the development of WGH down the years, and the improvements in health achieved. The exhibition stands were then taken round the district to all our out-stations in a 'Dispensary Week' of health promotion activities and preaching.

Elsie Ludlow retires

Our Matron, Elsie Ludlow, had been determined to see Independence in before she finally retired, completing thirty-one years 1929–1960. Her length of service was to be matched only by James and Hezekiah. Elsie's contribution had been recognized by the British authorities in 1955 with the award from the Queen of an MBE. She had provided a unique continuity through the years of change from Dr Hunter's time to Independence. David Cannon and I had shared eight years with her, and sometimes differed in our judgements, but always respected her consistency, especially in nursing matters. Her unfailing good humour and gift of seeing the funny side relieved many serious situations. She was slight of build, but of amazing stamina. She never had a day in bed off sick in all her thirty-one years, except for three weeks in her penultimate tour when the doctors insisted she had time off for a strained back. At her send-off in November 1960 mention was made of '...her unselfishness, her lack of pride, and her willingness to serve in any capacity. How many times has one of the doctors had to do a late emergency operation in the small hours, and Miss Ludlow, finding the theatre short of staff, would come on duty herself, not necessarily to give the anaesthetic, or to be first assistant, but simply to be an extra hand, and to help watch over the patient in case anything should be needed. It was invariably the patient first. Miss Ludlow is a true nurse, and a true follower of Our Lord.'

Years later, one of the nurses whom she trained said 'Sometimes at Ilesha we thought we were hard done by, and things were tough. Now we realise we had the best training anywhere in Nigeria, and others recognize that too.'

Recruiting staff

Now that we had a relatively permanent core team of long-service doctors, it was possible also to fit in others coming for short terms, each making their own special contribution. Dr Elizabeth Kendrew came to us for five months in 1958. Dr Kay MacWilliam, MRCP, DCH came for a tour 1959–1960, caring mainly for medical cases. She was the daughter of Dr E U MacWilliam, the pioneer builder of the old hospital in the 1920s, and born two years after he left. The Ilesha people were delighted to see her, and called her 'Omowale' - 'daughter come home'. Dr Fred Follett followed Kay at the end of 1960, driving from Wenchi Hospital in Ghana where he had been doing another locum. Dr Ann Musson helped for two months in early 1961, allowing David Morley to spend full time on analysing his research figures. Dr Alan Kerr, from Belfast, came for six months in August 1962 to cover for surgery while Dr Goonewardene went on leave. We were rich in help from all sides.

Some came as missionaries, others as *missionary associates,* accepting the same rate of pay as missionaries but with the hospital responsible for salary, allowances and fares, not the church in Britain. The pay was often considerably less than they had been receiving at home, and less than half the professional level in Nigeria, but there was a steady stream of those prepared to make that sacrifice and come. On the field, whether missionary or missionary associate, we were all one team together. The Methodist Church Nigeria recognized both types of worker in its Constitution, and both came only in response to an invitation from the President, as well as with the support of the MMS, the hospital, and the Ministry of Health, Ibadan.

We did our best to obtain Nigerian doctors, but there seemed all too few of them - only 1000 for a country of 35 million people - and we were not successful, despite offering the national rate for the job. Many nurses trained in Britain were now returning and we were able to recruit some as Sisters. Our first hospital worker to be sent overseas for higher training was Mr Amos Ajayi, laboratory technologist. He went for a year to work for his Finals of the Institute of Medical Laboratory Technology, but later disappointed us. The drive for well qualified local staffing was never far from our minds.

Our first pharmacist was a missionary, Miss Kathleen Owen MPS,and she relieved the doctors of the responsibility for all drug ordering and supply. She also took on the supervision of a Central Sterile Supply Department recently completed between the pharmacy office and the Operating Theatre. She launched the hospital on its own production of intravenous infusion fluids and sterile giving sets, for which silicone paper ('baking parchment') was used very effectively as the wrapping - a suggestion of John Mellanby's. The paper was water-proof but could be penetrated by steam during sterilisation.

A 'Plan of Development'

Chief S L Akintola, Premier for the Western Region government visited in April 1960, and expressed his 'deep appreciation of the tremendous and useful work being done', and mentioned in passing that his Government intended to set aside £40,000 for the extension of the hospital by 60 beds in the 1960–65 Regional Development Plan. This was later confirmed in writing, and more definite plans for expansion were set in motion. By this time the loan from the Blaize Institute had been paid off, and we were free to look to the future.

The plans for the new 'Glaxo Hostel' arrived from Brian Searle in April. This was the last building for which he was architect, but what a great contribution he had made! Our immediate question was, where should the hostel be sited? Our answer came through Mr Ron Morling, a Methodist friend from the Town Planning Department in Ibadan, who came to spend Easter 1960 with us, and give us a week of his time. He brought his surveying equipment and proceeded first to check up on the original site survey, and correctly map the position of all buildings put up so far. Then he sketched out a suggested 'Plan of Development' allocating sites for extending the wards, maternity department, outpatients', X-ray, nursing school, nurses' home, staff residences and, last but not least, the Medical Students' Hostel. The essential new feeder roads on his plan were built at once, and the Hostel commenced. The remaining extensions were all to become fact over the next twelve years. Few hospitals have had such an orderly and functional plan to work to. There is a tendency to tack on bits here and there as new demands arise. WGH Ilesha was saved from that, at least until 1975, through the timely help of Ron Morling.

When the Governor of the Western Region, Sir Adesoji Aderemi, visited Ilesha in February 1961 he opened the Medical Students Hostel, and named it Jephcott House. The Chairman of Glaxo's Jephcott Trust, Sir Harry Jephcott, allowed his name to be used for a building for the first time. The hostel was to prove a tremendous asset, not just in housing students, but in providing accommodation for junior doctors, and other visitors. Sir Harry and Lady Jephcott came themselves to view it in 1966.

Another task performed by the Governor on his visit in 1961 was to press the button to start the new high-efficiency steam autoclave installed by Allen and Hanburys for the CSSD. It looked good, but it soon showed us that it had problems. It was of a new type which blew a whistle every time something went wrong. We called it 'Ernie', and Ernie was not very popular. The makers had not realised the problems of running such a

Fig 5.1 *Building Jephcott House in 1960*

Fig 5.2 *Sir Harry and Lady Jephcott visit Ilesha*

machine in the tropics where the water is not clean, the steam pressure low, and the electricity supply likely to vary in voltage, lose a phase or go off completely at any time. Twice engineers were sent from England, but they failed to find a permanent answer. It was not until John Mellanby came and stayed long enough to diagnose all the problems, and cure all of Ernie's faults one by one, that the machine settled down and stopped blowing its alarm! Then it was fine. How many hospitals in the tropics, before and since, have been landed with equipment which has not been fully tested for service in hard conditions!

Morley child health methods spread to out-stations

To cover Margaret Woodland's leave in 1960 we had Sister Jean Wingfield working at Imesi. She did so well that, after Margaret's return in September she was given the task of converting all our dispensaries in the

Ilesha area to the Under Fives Clinic system, and the use of growth charts. A team went with her for a campaign of health education and community development.

To accommodate the new system at our branch Maternity Hospital in Ikole, a new out-patient department was built in 1961 according to plans drawn up by Dr David Cannon. It was put up by a local builder, and turned out much bigger than we expected. There was some speculation that perhaps the builder had interpreted feet as yards! However, the space was all useful. One tragedy occurred that year. Sister Helena Kohler who had been recruited for Ikole, had only been out four months when she came down with severe jaundice due to an acute fulminating hepatitis. She was brought to Ilesha, and only then did we discover that she had long had asthma which was controlled only by oral steroids. She was not a safe risk in the tropics, but her condition had not been made known before coming. With compromised immunity she died in a few days, and was buried in the Methodist church-yard near the old hospital.

One should perhaps pause to note that this was the only missionary death on the field related to service at WGH Ilesha and its out-stations in all its years. Many picked up illnesses - amoebic dysentery, malaria, filariasis loa-loa, onchocerciasis, tuberculosis, infective hepatitis, poliomyelitis, temporary mental breakdown - a long list of conditions; but all were treated, and none proved fatal, except this one. What a contrast to the frequent loss of missionary life in the nineteenth century when these health hazards were not understood and so much more dangerous!

In early 1961, when the Methodist Church planned a new advance into Borgu in the Northern Region using a combined approach with church outreach, agriculture, and health care, Dr Morley proposed that the health side be through a Maternity Centre and Under Fives Clinic. The Fund for Human Need gave a grant to make the initiative possible, and I had the task of preparing plans for the first Under Fives Clinic to be purpose-built from the start. We were of course building on the health work already pioneered in the area for twenty-five years by the Ludlows. The goodwill and community understanding had been established. The Emir of Borgu was very happy to grant land for a new centre at Kaiama, and on my next visit I took some striped poles and 100-foot measuring tape to survey the site and fix the corner posts. The Health Centre and

Sister's House were both designed around large underground tanks, and rain water from every roof slope was ducted into these. It was arid country, with rain for only three months in the year, but it was hoped the system would collect enough in that time to last through the nine months of dry. And it did! Water was lifted by a semi-rotary pump to a galvanized tank in the roof-space from where it flowed by gravity to wash-basins and water closets as required. Life in this very rural area was made tolerable for Sister Jean Wingfield who moved in to take charge, with a doctor's visit from Ilesha once a quarter. Helping Sister was Mr Stephen Oshiobugie, trained as a dresser and health educator by the Ludlows, and known as 'The Happy Man' because of his unfailing smile. Sister Margaret Brigg, and others followed, and after the completion of the Kainji Dam across the River Niger in 1970, another fine health centre was built in the new town of New Bussa and the supervising sister moved from Kaiama to open it in 1972. This centre replaced the clinic which the Ludlows had started in 'old' Bussa, now submerged beneath Kainji Lake. Michael, one of Stephen's ten children in Kaiama, was later to work at Ilesha as an accounts clerk, while his twin sister, Mary, trained as a nurse. Michael went on to offer for the Methodist Ministry and is now a well-known bishop of that church.

Measles vaccine research

David Morley's work was certainly progressing well, but there was one infectious disease for which his Under Fives Clinics system did not provide a sufficient answer, and that was measles. It was very infectious, even before the rash appeared, and caused such serious complications. The age of onset varied from six months to two years, with an average of 14 months - and the children got it badly. One in twenty died. What should we do? An unexpected opportunity then occurred. David heard that in the United States a vaccine against measles was being given provisional trials. At the end of 1960 he invited the team of doctors developing the Enders vaccine to come and do the pilot trials at Imesi-Ile where the effects could be closely observed and followed up. Dr Saul Krugman (assisted later by Dr Sam Katz) brought the vaccine from the States packed in 'dry ice', and it was given to twenty-five children, the first in the African continent to receive it. Twenty-five were matched with them as controls. The Cannon's two children, Peter and Elizabeth, and our two out at that time, Alison and Bryan, also received vaccine, the first European children to be inoculated. Results showed complete protection for all those vaccinated (including our four), though some had fever for a few days and a fleeting rash. Among the twenty-five controls there were the usual number of cases, and some deaths. Two years later a further modified vaccine giving less reaction was available, and David returned for a short while to complete his research. The vaccine was used for all Imesi children from July 1962 to 1965, and at the end of that time the results showed that Imesi-Ile had become the first village in the world to be freed from the scourge of measles. General release then carried the benefits world-wide.

Dr Morley retires, but continues his work from London

In June 1961 David Morley completed his five years as agreed with WACMR and WGH Ilesha, returned to England, and joined the staff of London University. He was eventually invited to set up a Tropical Child Health Unit in the Institute of Child Health, the 'medical school' of Great Ormond Street Children's Hospital, and Margaret Woodland joined him to repeat the Imesi partnership. In January 1963 Dr Morley was invited to the Royal Society of Medicine to present the initial findings of his research at Imesi-Ile, and the background to his ideas about Under Fives Clinics. His paper published under the title 'A medical service for children under five years of age in West Africa' (1) was strategically important in establishing his role. He was able to run UNICEF/WHO supported courses for students of Nutrition at the London School of Tropical Medicine, and several groups were brought to Ilesha for field experience. His ideas began to spread as ex-students found themselves promoted to key posts in government health ministries throughout the developing world. Many countries adopted the Under Fives Clinic approach, and had growth-charts printed in their own language. Ilesha began to be known internationally. In 1965 a request for more information about 'the Morley system' came from Albert Schweitzer's old hospital at Lambarene! Zambia issued a stamp in 1971 with a design depicting a child being weighed at an Under Fives Clinic.

An important landmark was a book which came out of a conference in Makerere, Uganda, organized by Professor Maurice King, in which Dr Morley played a key part. In 1965 Professor King, a microbiologist, had done a locum in a bush mission hospital for his friend Dr Peter C.V. Cox. Maurice found so many problems of medicine and surgery, and, in general, just how to run a hospital in the tropics, for which there were no published answers. He realised there was a gap to fill. The conference on 'Health Centres and Hospitals in Africa', called with WHO/UNICEF backing in Makerere in 1966, provided all the material for his book *Medical Care in Developing Countries* (2). Much of it came from Dr Morley out of his Ilesha and Imesi-Ile experience, and he was given a vision of what was needed world-wide. Professor King sent a complementary copy of his book to me at Ilesha 'with apologies that it was so much Ilesha'. The book proved to be the first of a whole new genre of books for doctors in small hospitals and health centres throughout the developing world on every relevant subject - Primary Child Care, Primary Surgery, District Health Care, Ophthalmology for Developing countries, and so on through all the specialities. Dr Morley's own book on *Paediatric Priorities in the Developing World* 1973 (3), was one of the early ones. Mine on *Medical administration for front-line doctors,* 1990 (4), based mainly on WGH Ilesha experience, was very much later but in the same line.

The paediatric succession at WGH

Taking over from Dr Morley was not easy. Just before he went, Dr Jonathan Hartfield arrived, recruited by the MMS. His special interest was obstetrics, but as David Cannon was still with us he gladly agreed to do the paediatrics, and succeeded brilliantly, carrying on the Morley methods. When Dr Wesley Clapp, a specialist paediatrician from America finally arrived, a year after David's departure, he found it hard to adapt to methods which contrasted so much with what he was used to in California, and left after one year. Thereafter the child health side of the hospital was manned by short-term staff, Dr Ping Pang (a Chinese Methodist) - four months, Dr Michael Orme - two months, Dr Joan Bicknell, who was in Nigeria and answered a local advertisement - five months and Dr Michael Weeks - nine months. For 1966 I had to be Acting Paediatrician myself, which was a challenge, but an enjoyable one. I was given some part-time help by Dr Nick Cunningham, an American paediatrician doing research. Subsequent specialists to take on the job were Dr Marthe Le Dune - 1967 (she, unfortunately, had to return home ill after nine months); Dr Maureen Duggan - 1968–1969 (intense, dedicated and a born linguist, picking up Yoruba with all the correct tones just by listening to her patients), Dr Brian McGucken - 1973 (his wife, Dr Frances McGucken, also helped part-time), Dr Mary Thwaites 1970–1975 (later to marry Mr Beyer the laboratory superintendent) and Dr Jenny Mee - 1974–1975. Despite all these staff changes, the style of child health care that Dr Morley showed to be effective was maintained. Much of the recruitment was done through personal contacts, though with help from the Methodist Missionary Society whenever they found it possible.

The Deans

One story of recruitment was unusual. While on leave in England I was invited to speak at an overseas missionary meeting at a church in Coleshill, east of Birmingham. The chairman for the occasion was Dr Dennis Dean, a local general practitioner. Over a meal afterwards he mentioned that he would like his practice to give some assistance to medical missionary work. What would I suggest? It turned out that both he and his wife, also a GP, would really like to come and work themselves, so I said 'Why not?' It took a year to arrange things with their partners, and in that time Dennis completed his studies for the MRCP. He also spent time at the East Birmingham hospital obtaining general surgical experience and learning how to repair an inguinal hernia. Dr Iona Dean, his wife, brushed up on her practical obstetrics and learned how to do a Caesarean section. They found a locum to stand in for them for a year, Dr Weeks, and arranged for his payment to be on their account. In 1963 they came, together with their two sons, John and Peter, and a girl, Pauline, who was between leaving school and starting nursing. She was able to release Iona from some of her family responsibility so that she could work full-time alongside Dennis. Both enjoyed the experience to the full - and their practice colleagues in Castle Bromwich entered into the spirit of the link-up with Ilesha. The second partner and his wife came out for a holiday, as did the practice secretary/receptionist. When my wife and I were due for leave in July 1963, Dennis said, 'You are welcome to use the Dean house in Castle Bromwich, as long you do not mind looking after the locum'. We had previously had to use the Missionary Guest House flats in Selly Oak, Birmingham, but with four growing children this was becoming increasingly difficult, so we gladly accepted. At the end of our six months break (three months holiday and three months 'on deputation', travelling round the country speaking about the work overseas in Methodist churches and conferences) Dr Michael Weeks asked if we could use him in Ilesha too! Again, the offer was accepted and Mike came out as the Deans returned, and stayed for two very useful years.

The obstetricians

After opening the new Ante-natal Clinic in 1959 David Cannon and his maternity staff found that attendances of ante-natal patients began to escalate, rising from 14,000 a year to 17,000 in 1960. Confinements rose from 950 to 1400, and our 26-bed maternity ward was overcrowded. There was no prospect then of a new and larger unit. However there

Fig 5.3 *The Dean Family*

Fig 5.4 *Dr and Mrs Jonathan Hartfield and family (March 1971)*

were six private maternity homes in the town, staffed by midwives whom we ourselves had trained and of proved competence. David inspected their premises, approved them as adequate, and offered the homes free medical supervision if they would accept referred cases from the hospital in which a normal delivery could be expected. Fee levels were seen to be reasonable. It was to be a new an important experiment in cooperation with the private sector. The midwives were instructed as to which cases they should refer for hospital care. At the hospital ante-natal patients who were found to have no 'high-risk factors' were given the choice of hospital or maternity home delivery (the latter costing a little less), and many very sensibly chose the latter. By 1962 the hospital Antenatal Clinic attendances had dropped to 14,000 again, and the confinements to 1200. Dr Cannon and Dr Hartfield reported jointly in 1964 (5) on the results of the first five years of the scheme. 1032 births had been supervised in the private maternity homes, during which there had been no maternal deaths and only 37 stillbirths. 54 patients had been transferred to the hospital. The results, within the context of the usual poor level of health care in the developing world, were sufficiently remarkable to be commented on in a *Lancet* editorial (6). The good work continued under Dr Iona Dean, Dr Michael Cox and the other obstetricians who followed on.

The surgical succession

Dr Roy Goonewardene left in January 1964, and initially worked at the government General Hospital in Abeokuta, with the hopes of earning enough to set up a small hospital for himself in his home country, Sri Lanka. Plans did not work out, and he and his family emigrated to Australia. Finding a surgical successor for WGH was not easy. Dr Michael Cox arrived in February 1964. He was an MMS missionary obstetrician who had already done three tours at Queen Elizabeth Hospital, Umuahia, in the east of Nigeria. He and his wife, Ursula, stayed for two years, and Michael, from his wide experience, helped cover for surgery until Dr Osmund Mulligan arrived in November. Osmund and Sylvia, also Methodist missionaries, were from Northern Ireland, but had served some years in eastern Nigeria under the Qua-Iboe Mission, at Annang Joint Hospital. They had in fact called at WGH Ilesha for a night on their way from Annang to Lagos in February 1962, and we were able to find their picture in our Visitors' Book when we heard they were coming. Osmund made one condition, that he be allowed three months to learn the Yoruba language, and this we were pleased to accept. My father, Dr

George Pearson, who was on his way home from doing a locum at the Methodist Hospital at Wenchi, Ghana, stayed with us in Nigeria, and took surgical calls for the period Osmund was studying. It was good to have our missionary medical team up to full strength again. Osmund was to make an outstanding contribution to WGH and the Ilesha community, both as a surgeon and as a preacher.

Electives

Useful insights into the health needs in developing countries was also given to many senior medical students through the medium of 'elective postings', which were becoming increasingly popular in medical schools around the world. The first to come were a pair from Birmingham and Bristol medical schools in 1960. In 1962 we had a student from the United States, and also Mr Paul Snell from UK, recommended to us by the MMS. Paul was later to become the first Medical Superintendent of Dabou Methodist Hospital in Cote d'Ivoire, built in 1964 to commemorate the centenary of Methodist medical work overseas. A succession of 'electives' followed from all over the world. They brought a fascinating variety to our company in Ilesha, and took back valuable impressions of the needs and opportunities in developing country medicine. Some felt they would never be the same again.

Autonomy for the Methodist Church, and Fiftieth Jubilee celebrations for WGH Ilesha

Two years on from Independence for Nigeria came autonomy for the Methodist Church Nigeria. The two previous Districts of the British Methodist Church in Western Nigeria and Eastern Nigeria were united under one Methodist Conference, independent of Britain, but with a fraternal relationship. October 1962 was also celebrated as WGH Ilesha's 50th Jubilee. All was set for an open-air meeting, but at the last minute, down came the rain, and everybody had to squash inside the hospital chapel as best they could. The Vice-President of the new Conference was there, many Nigerian ministers, and the Rev. Philip Potter from the MMS in London, but the national nature of the occasion was shown by the presence of professors of paediatrics from Ibadan and Lagos, Secretary of the Nigeria Nursing Council, Chairman of Nigeria Airways, and Lady Head, wife of the British High Commissioner. Mark Okunsanya, Dr Stephens' assistant, was there to speak, and also Dr Joyce Ludlow with her vivid story of the first midwife going to Imesi-Ile. I brought the WGH story up-to-date. Between speeches a nurses choir, with drummers, sang

Yoruba lyrics composed for the occasion by Methodist minister and musician, Rev Ola Olude, and the day concluded with drama, food and a football match!

On January 12th 1963 we continued the Jubilee celebrations, remembering the actual day when Dr Stephens first arrived in Ilesha. This time the President of Conference, Methodist Church Nigeria was present. There was a procession through the town, and funds were raised for a new 400 m.a. X-ray machine, and extension of consulting-room space in the Outpatient Department. Dr Azikwe, Governor-General of Nigeria, contributed £100.

Save the Children Fund unit

An extension of Dr Morley's community child health work began in 1963 when the charity organization, Save the Children Fund (SCF), began stationing health visitors in Imesi. Joyce Martin came first, and was visited by Lady Metcalfe from SCF headquarters in London. Joyce had to return home after a few months but was followed by Jean Stewart, daughter of Rev John Stewart, the very one who had married Gwladys Charlesworth, the first nurse at Ilesha! She was another to be warmly welcomed as 'Omowale', 'Child come home'. SCF was keen to have its own unit, based in Ilesha. The leprosy village land next to the old hospital had been vacant for six years, but fear of the disease prevented the Council from reclaiming the area. At my request, Dr Goldie of the Baptist Leposarium in Ogbomosho, seventy miles away, came to inspect and to issue a document declaring the land free from infection. The Council therefore allowed SCF free use of it for ten years. Housing for staff was put up, and garaging for vehicles and a store. Sister Ossai and an Administrator, Capt. Brown joined the team, and SCF began a valuable mobile work throughout the district. Initially WGH informed the health visitors whenever a recovered kwashiorkor case was ready to go back home. The Sisters picked up the mother and child, transported them to their village, and invariably met with a warm welcome, as a child given up for lost was restored to the community. Health and nutrition education from the Sisters was listened to carefully, and the mother, who had seen what foods and therapy had brought her child through, was able to be the teacher to the others. Before long the SCF had forty village centres to which they toured, becoming known as the 'Sisters with the car'. Ibadan medical students who were taken out to see their work were impressed. 'We have often talked to patients about nutrition' one said, 'but we have never actually seen what went into the cooking pot before.' In 1974 the whole work was handed over to the Local Government. Remi Domingo, the SCF Sister from 1968, married the king, the Owa-Obokun of Ijeshaland, so was entitled to be called 'Olori' (Queen). She moved to work with the Local Government, and developed the SCF work as a mothercraft and 'Multipurpose' centre.

A Home Gardens project

An extension of this work for improved nutrition came in May 1966 when the Food and Agriculture Organization (FAO) of the United Nations was invited by the government of Nigeria to establish in Ilesha a 'Home Gardens for Improved Nutrition' project in Ilesha. It was part of FAO's 'Freedom from Hunger Campaign'. The idea was to encourage householders and farmers to grow useful foods close to their homes, other than the usual staple foods of maize, yam and cassava. At the central model garden on the Ministry of Agriculture land at Imo, outside the town, every known traditional food plant was studied and nutritive content analysed to see which of them were good in protein or vitamins. Other common plants were also looked at to see if new foods could be found with acceptable taste. Recipe books were prepared, and seed packets made up for distribution throughout the region. My wife gave the centre cuttings from our mulberry bushes which we had obtained from Dr Stanley Browne in Uzuakoli. He had first introduced them to Nigeria from Zaire. The Project spread them round Western Nigeria. It was fascinating to see some of the thirty-five vegetable plants and forty fruit trees, and to note the fifty pests and plant diseases which had been tackled. Reports were produced in 1969, 1971 and 1973 (7) but I am not aware that the Nigerian government did anything with the mine of information that was made available, or continued the seed distribution and promotion of home gardens.

Imesi-Ile and Oke-Mesi compared

In October 1966 the American paediatrician, Dr Nicholas Cunningham began his important study to cross-check on Dr Morley's work. He compared the community of Imesi-Ile with its Under Five Clinic, with another community 6 miles away as the crow-flies, Oke-Mesi. Because of the mountainous terrain the only link was by a road of over 20 miles. Oke-Mesi had a traditional Local Authority dispensary/maternity, and was blessed with piped water. Imesi-Ile still depended on wells, with all the hazards of possible pollution. For 12 months Dr Cunningham studied the progress of children in both villages, and found that the Imesi-Ile children were, by all accepted indications (infant mortality, toddler weight, height etc) significantly healthier. He concluded that the Under Fives Clinic had indeed made the difference, and his important research was later published in *The Journal of Tropical Paediatrics* (6).

More enquiries about the Under Fives Clinic system began to come in from America, and elsewhere in Africa. In 1975 the concept was 'wholeheartedly accepted' by a joint committee of WHO and UNICEF.

Children's Ward extensions with Oxfam aid

A suggested extension to the WGH Children's Ward had been sketched out by Dr Morley before he left in 1961, but it was not until we secured grants from Oxfam that we were able to build it. In conformity with David's ideas, the design allowed for the mother and child to be together, but in cubicled sections of four cots, to reduce cross-infection, the cubicles being divided by glass windows for easy observation from the nurses' station. For the sanitary facilities, there was one room where the nurses could organize the nappy laundry, and another beside it where the mothers could empty and clean potties, and have a toilet for themselves. The building was officially opened in March 1967 as the first public duty of the newly installed king, Owa Agunlejika. The mothers and their children, who were moved in from the side verandahs of the old ward where they had been 'making do', were radiant and cheerful to have proper accommodation at last. They were given a colourful blouse and wrapper as 'uniform', and one visitor, catching sight of the mothers through successive glass partitions from the nurses desk exclaimed, 'They look like angels'. Tim Brierley, an Oxfam field organizer, wrote afterwards,

> 'Congrats on putting up such a beautiful and original building with our grant .....quite the nicest building I have seen constructed with Oxfam money'.

Dr Marthe LeDune, the first specialist paediatrician to follow Dr Morley, arrived just in time for the ward opening. We were so glad to see her, but she brought tragic news from her home town, Newcastle, UK, where the Oxfam money had been raised. With the help of the local paper, the Evening Chronicle, Oxfam organized a sponsored Charity Walk, the

Fig 5.5 *Hurford Ward, opened 1969*

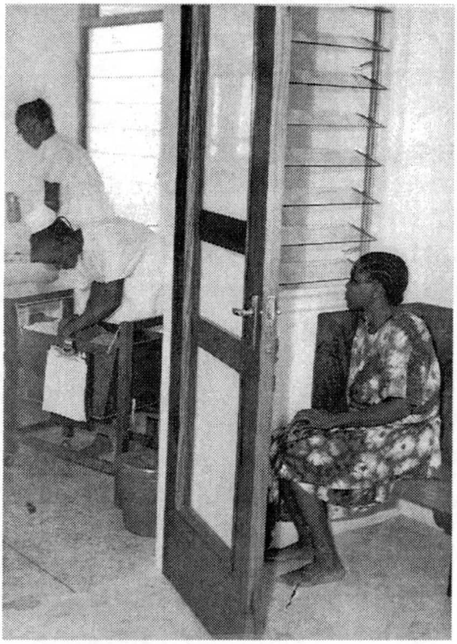

Fig 5.6 *Mr and Mrs Hurford, and their two remaining children, flown out for the official opening of Hurford Ward*

first of its kind, scheduled to start at mid-night from the Newcastle United football stadium. 6,000 were expected, each to raise £1, but to everyone's surprise 12,000 turned up! Fifteen minutes before mid-night a reporter opened the big gates to get his car inside, then closed them again. The crowd thought the Walk had started and surged against the closed gates in the darkness. Thirty were injured in the crush, and one 17-year old girl, Margaret Hurford, died that night. The melee was sorted out, the Walk went on and not £6,000, but £26,000 was raised! None knew of the death till the following day, but new regulations controlling such walks were introduced.

Two years later a second phase of the Oxfam-funded extension was built, a special ward for premature babies. At Oxfam's request it was named 'Hurford Ward' in memory of the girl that had died. The opening was in February 1969, and Margaret Hurford's parents, and two other children in the family, were funded to come out for the occasion by an anonymous donor. Actually, they nearly missed the ceremony because of travel delays caused by freezing fog in the U.K., and reached Lagos with just 2 hours to go. However, a business friend in Lagos, who knew the urgency, chartered a four-seater plane and a pilot, and phoned up saying that all he wanted was an aerodrome! We replied, 'Make for Oshogbo', an RAF airfield left over from the war which still had a skeleton staff and a wind-sock. Mrs Pearson raced over with the hospital van, met and brought the party, somewhat dazed, but just in time. People were very moved by this brave family, who had lost a daughter, but who were happy to see other children's lives being saved through her sacrifice. The ward we had built was of unique design based on specifications I gave to the architect. These were a compromise between the Morley principle of the mother being with the child all the time, and the usual premature ward principle (as at the teaching hospital in Ibadan), of trying to isolate the baby in a sterile environment till its own immune processes could resist infection. The mother was kept at a distance and nurses with masks and gloves provided the care. At the centre of the Hurford Ward was the sterile nursing area with access to the glass-walled baby cubicles on either side. A second door on the other side of the cubicle gave the mother access as soon as the nurse decided it was safe. In practice this was usually from the start, so that the mother would not lose the stimulus to lactation, and the baby would benefit from her touching. The mother was no longer excluded from caring for her own child, and the advantages far outweighed any added risk. The system worked well.

A visitor from the U.K. Medical Research Council in 1969, Dr Murray Baker, commented after being shown round that he thought we had a model hospital.

> 'Of all the places in the world that I have been to', he said, 'I cannot think of another which could give a doctor greater job-satisfaction.'

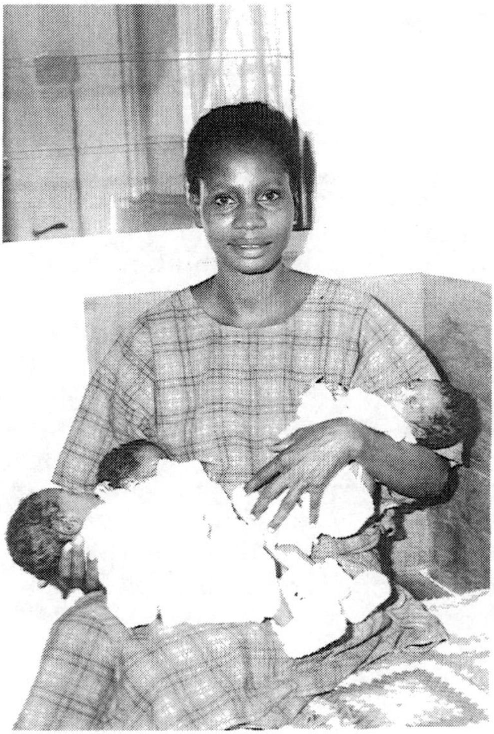

Fig 5.7 *Mother of triplets successfully cared for in Hurford Ward*

CHAPTER 6

AN EXPANDING SERVICE

Clinical interests

Encouraging research
Ilesha was definitely on the map, both for people within Nigeria and from many parts of the world. We had a continual succession of fascinating visitors. Among them, though not until 1971, was Dr Dennis Burkitt, known to the medical world through 'Burkitt's lymphoma', that strange tumour in children causing swellings of the jaw and in the abdomen which he first described through his work in Kenya. He was also known for his advocacy of a high-fibre diet for Europeans. Many diseases in Africa were rare, he claimed, because people naturally ate a diet rich in fibre, with more rapid transit of digested food through the bowels. Appendicitis, diverticulitis and colonic cancer were all rare as a result, but common in the west with its diet of low-fibre and highly processed food. He had a good case, and all expatriates who heard him immediately added brown bread or All Bran to their diet, 'just in case'! Dennis had travelled widely throughout Africa, particularly going to hospitals in rural areas, and learning as he went. From this experience he used to say,

> 'Every bush doctor is a world expert in the diseases of his area'.

'Ijesha shakes'
In WGH Ilesha we certainly had a wide variety of clinical problems on which to apply our medical curiosity. Paediatrics was a major interest, as it should be in a continent where 50% of the population was aged fourteen years or under, but child health was not our only concern. Perhaps the earliest published paper from Ilesha came from Dr Wright and Dr Morley (1) on a condition they called 'Encephalitis tremens'. This was a strange disease which occurred in epidemics of forty to fifty

cases from August to December each year. Many were children aged five to nine years, but it also occurred in adults up to seventy years, with an average age of onset at twenty-five. Quite suddenly they would start with vomiting, giddiness and an 'intention tremor' of the arms. This caused violent shaking, for example if patients tried to put a hand to their mouth, and many could not walk without staggering. Theories blaming it on the eating of 'new yams', or on the pesticides sprayed on cocoa trees, were never proved. It might have been a virus infection, but we had no proof of that either. Nearly all the patients came from Ilesha town, but some from the surrounding villages, so we informally called it 'Ijesha shakes'. Both patients and their relatives were very alarmed by the gross tremor, so cases were admitted for observation. Fortunately most recovered, with minimal therapy, in about 4 days. With the help of the Virus Research Laboratory at University College Hospital, Ibadan, an effort was made to isolate a virus, but without success (2). Professor B O Oshuntokun, of Ibadan, was prepared to mount a bigger study, but despite the fact that the epidemic had come regularly for twenty years, the 1973 cases never appeared, and the disease petered out. Was it because of the severe African drought of 1973 which dried up all the grass in Ilesha area for six months instead of the usual three and brought the Sahara desert 100 miles further south into the Sahel? Such a climatic change may have affected an insect carrier of the disease, and recent evidence supports this. But who knows? I did see a case or two in Igbo-ora four years later, and no-one there had met this strange disease before!

Malaria, typhoid, symphysiotomy and much else

Dr David Cannon did a study on the effects of malaria on pregnant mothers, and showed that those who had malaria parasites in their placentae (the after-birth) produced babies on average half a pound lighter than those who were protected (3). Regular preventive anti-malaria therapy through the ante-natal period was therefore shown to be an advantage. All kinds of opportunities were taken for investigating local conditions, childhood tuberculosis (4), twinning rates in Yoruba women (remarkably high) (5), measles (very severe) (6), the place of symphysiotomy (a small operative procedure which enlarges the pelvis) in obstructed labour (7), and typhoid fever in young children (8). Dr Hartfield's important work on family planning methods showed how nurse/midwives could be taught to do insertions of IUCDs (the intrauterine contraceptive device) with results as good as those achieved by the doctor (9).

Skin colour in tuberculosis, and fractured femur healing
Studies which claimed my attention while at Ilesha included the change in skin colour which tends to occur when a patient gets tuberculosis. Patients on average become lighter, but return to their normal darker colour after treatment (10,11). The change is not related to anaemia (12). I reported on toxic reactions of patients in our TB clinic when treated with thiacetazone (13), and, as a tropical generalist, I also took an interest in fractured femur cases, because it seemed that patients got better so much more quickly in Nigeria than in Britain. A retrospective survey of 100 cases treated over twenty years by different doctors did in fact show that clinical union (healing of the bones together) occurred on average at 6–8 weeks, not 12–14 weeks as was the received wisdom of most orthopaedic specialists (14). However, one of them, Richard Batten, who was then at the Birmingham Accident Hospital, but was formerly at University College Hospital, Ibadan, made sure the article was published.

Public health - smallpox and cholera
On public health issues the hospital contributed a great deal through its child health clinics, and its cooperation with the Save the Children Fund team. From time to time other opportunities occurred to work more directly with the Ministry of Health for all age groups in the population. During the 1950s and early 60s, small-pox was still rampant, and the priests of Shopona, the small-pox god, were greatly feared. As soon as cases were diagnosed at WGH they were taken to a so-called 'Infectious Disease Hospital' on the town outskirts. Ilesha had one on the Akure road - little more than a well-ventilated barn. Perhaps it is still there. When in use, it was just a holding centre, with one caretaker/ dispenser in charge, but patients could rest there while the disease took its course. There was only palliative treatment. Some died, a few lost their sight, and all who survived were left with pox scars, particularly on the face. WGH staff shared in the local vaccination campaigns, helping to man road-blocks to catch the travellers. Small-pox vaccine was given to all children coming to hospital, but it was not until 1967 that the hospital was called to assist with the major campaign throughout Africa and the world, backed by WHO, which finally eliminated the disease. From 1980 no single case has occurred.

Cholera is still around and liable to cause explosive outbreaks where sanitation is poor, and where people depend on wells, creeks and water-holes for their drinking water supply. The last major epidemic in Nigeria which I saw was at the end of 1970, and was particularly serious in the big cities of Lagos, Kano and Ibadan and around the Niger delta. At its height, Eleta Catholic mission hospital in Ibadan was admitting up to 300 cases a day. With extra volunteers putting up intravenous drips as fast as they could. Amazingly, the death rate was kept down to only 3%!. In Ilesha the epidemic was not so bad, but the Isolation Ward was turned over to cholera alone, and about 250 cases were treated. A new medical journal arrived from London in January 1971 called *Tropical Doctor* and its first leading article was from Dr R N Chaudhury of Calcutta on 'Treatment of cholera'. The journal could not have been more welcome, and reminded us of how much could be done with oral rehydration fluid after the initial total collapse had been overcome by intravenous therapy.

Training

Another area in which WGH Ilesha was closely linked to national health concerns was in training. The training of nurses and midwives has been mentioned, and will be returned to. Other health personnel were also included such as laboratory technologists and pharmacy assistants.

Pre-registration doctors
In 1961 the hospital was inspected by three London consultants who had been external examiners at the Ibadan medical school MB.BS examinations. They reported favourably, and in 1962 the paediatric department of the hospital was recognized by the Nigeria Medical Council for the posting of doctors who needed six months of paediatrics during their 'Pre-registration Year'. Previously doctors stayed in their teaching hospital for this year. The first to come to us was Dr J B Familusi, later to become a Professor of Paediatrics in Lagos. A year later we welcomed Dr Sam A Olowe, who also went into paediatrics and became Chief Medical Director of Lagos University Teaching Hospital. He nearly returned to take charge at WGH in 1975. A continual succession of these 'junior house officers' followed, and in 1970 the hospital was recognized for surgery, obstetrics and medicine as well as paediatrics and we could take up to four doctors at a time.

Recognition of the hospital for post registration specialist surgical training also came in 1970. Dr D A Laosebikan was appointed in November that year as our first Surgical Registrar. He was later to qualify and take charge as surgeon at Oshogbo General Hospital, twenty miles away. Dr S Duvie was our second surgical registrar.

The rising standards of nurse training

The nurse training went through several stages of official recognition. As we have seen, the WGH Nursing School was recognized by the Nursing Council of Nigeria for the NRN (Nigerian Registered Nurse) training in 1950. Those who qualified in Britain, or at the University College Hospital, Ibadan, were recognized as SRN (State Registered Nurse). Sister Margaret Gardner took over as Nurse Tutor in 1961, and gradually raised the quality of training, and quantity too. At the end of 1962 there were seventy girls in training for both nursing and midwifery. Sister Doreen Habbershaw also arrived that year to help as Clinical Tutor. In 1964 the Nursing Council decided to raise the standards even further so that all Nigerian trained nurses could achieve the equivalent of SRN and receive international recognition. It was a big step. It meant that from 1964 all entrants had to be secondary school educated, no longer with just their Modern III Certificate. The training still proved popular and in December 1964, 3000 applied, 837 sat the entrance examination, and twenty-four only could be accepted. A new Nurses' Home, Ile-Esan, was completed in 1965 part paid for with funds from the Government's Development Plan, now dated 1962–1968. This additional block, with its twenty-four single or double rooms and a superb common room, was named after our HMC Chairman, the Rev. D.B.Esan, who had been such a staunch supporter of the hospital since his appointment to Ilesha Circuit. With the same government fund we had upgraded the hospital laundry with steam equipment, and built an excellent new X-ray department, spending £14,800 out of the £40,000 promised. Then the Ministry of Health's money ran out!

The government was in financial difficulties, and the expected grants were not forthcoming. Nearly all the additional buildings which were considered necessary if we were to continue with nurse training had to be put on hold. The exceptions were the two children's ward extensions which were Oxfam funded, an immunisation room extension in the outpatient department which was funded by the Jephcott Trust and a staff residence funded by the MMS. A new nursing school, extensions to the women's ward and a new maternity department, improvements to the operating theatre, a refrigerated mortuary, new administration block and three more staff residences, all had to wait. It did not look as if we would ever complete the Morling 'Development Plan', or even be able to continue nurse training.

Financial and political problems

Free treatment for children temporarily stopped
Difficulties then extended to our regular grants from government which accounted for 40% of our costs. These came mainly from the refunds for the treatment of children under the age of eighteen. As the numbers had progressively escalated, so had our claim for grant. In the second half of 1965, when I was on leave and Dr Michael Cox was Acting Medical Superintendent, the grants dried up and the hospital was sliding into debt at the rate of £1000 a week. In December, when the government was 12 months in arrears and our debts stood at £32,000, Dr Cox informed the Ministry, and put an advertisement in the local papers, to announce that the hospital would have to withdraw from the Free Treatment scheme.

On January 15th there was a military coup (unrelated to the hospital situation!), Prime Minister Tafewa Balewa was assassinated and General Ironsi, an Igbo soldier, took charge. By the time I arrived back on Jan 25th there was 'new management' at the Ministry, 'frozen assets' were released in mid-February, Free Treatment for children was restored, and Under Fives Clinic attendances shot up from 4,000 a month to the usual 12,000, and staff were busier than ever.

Uneasy relations with the government
That was not the end of the financial crisis. In July the government proposed cutting all grants to Voluntary Agency Hospitals, unless they came into a system of Combined Management. In principle the HMC of WGH accepted this, but suggested postponement to March 1967 till details of the new system could be worked out and the approval of our church proprietors obtained, Catholic, Anglican, Seventh Day Adventist and Methodist. The country remained unsettled.

At the end of July 1966 General Ironsi was killed by northern officers and General Gowon, a Christian from a minority northern group, was installed as Military Governor. The country was divided into six States in an effort to disperse the centres of power north and south. However, in September there was a catastrophic outbreak of violence against Igbos resident in the north. These ambitious, hardworking people had spread from the east all over the country as business men and professionals. Their success provoked jealousy among the Hausas. 2000 Igbos were killed, 5000 injured and a million fled from the north back to their eastern homeland. All efforts to obtain justice proved unavailing. Resentment grew. Feelings began to harden.

In the west of Nigeria life proceeded at local level without much change. No answers were received by the church proprietors from the Ministry of Health in Ibadan, and by November 10th we had to face bitter reality. With heavy debts growing the Under Fives free treatment was again reluctantly discontinued and adult fees put up 50%. Ilesha WGH's HMC reckoned this would still only cover one-third of the deficit so it was also decided that the hospital must give itself one month to complete negotiations with the government - or close. I had the unenviable job of issuing provisional letters of one month's notice of termination to every member of staff from the night-watchman to myself. That caused headlines in the national press, 'DOCTOR PEARSON SACKS 200', but within a week the Military Governor of the Western Region had called all the hospital authorities together, agreed to the temporary restoration of grants on the existing system until March 1968, and set up a small committee with representatives from government, missions (a Catholic sister/doctor and myself) and the community, with Professor T O Ogunlesi from College of Medicine, Ibadan, as the independent chairman. A new system of grant-aiding had to be devised, one that would meet the requirements of government auditors, and be fair to the voluntary agency hospitals that were providing at least one-third of the health services in the region. The 'Ogunlesi committee' met weekly from April to June. It was hard work. Dr Bayo Banjo (for the government side) and myself produced the critical formula for calculating grants which carried the day. The report was submitted but it was not until December that we heard that the proposals had been provisionally accepted. Formal acceptance and implementation of the new-style block grants began in July 1968 and were to prove a satisfactory basis for government aid and voluntary agency cooperation for the next ten years.

The Biafran civil war
During the first half of 1967, the majority of the easterners on WGH staff, said that their relatives had urged them to leave the West and return home. Throughout the country there was this exodus of people. Many of the refugees from the North came by train as far as Oshogbo, then travelled by buses or lorries through Ilesha to the east before borders were closed in June. Later that month Lt. Col Ojukwu unilaterally declared independence for the Eastern Region from the rest of Nigeria, and the area took the name 'Biafra'. Undoubtedly, the newly found oil reserves in the Niger river delta, much of it within the Eastern Region, was part of the reason for secession. French oil interests were strongly in support. General Gowon failed to secure a settlement by negotiation. The civil war began, and lasted three years.

It was a serious set-back for that part of Nigeria which was involved. This was not the whole country. The size of Biafra was similar to that of Wales, but set in a country four times the size of Britain. In the rest of Nigeria life continued much as normal, but the hardships within Biafra were cruel. It was the peasant farmers and their families who suffered most due to the movement of population and failure to grow enough food. Pictures of starving malnourished children caught the sympathy of the world. Judging from the west, and from Lagos, there was never the desire for genocide which the Igbos were told to fear, and which the international media echoed. When Ojukwu finally fled the country in early 1970, and General Effiong and Sir Louis Mbanefo (Chief Justice) brought Biafra's surrender to Gowon, they shook hands and declared the war had been 'a quarrel between brothers'. No heads rolled. The country came together again. Within a month the Igbo medical students who had missed out on their paediatric posting to Ilesha were back to take their turn. If only other countries could settle their civil wars so amicably!

Help from Holland

First contacts
In September of 1967 when Dr Hartfield was Acting Medical Superintendent, he received a visit from the Secretary of a Dutch aid organization, Interchurch Coordination Committee for Development Aid

(ICCO - from its Dutch initials), which was particularly interested in jointly funded projects with a major training component. He learned that Queen Elizabeth Hospital, Umuahia, was putting in a claim, but the unsettled situation in Eastern Nigeria had caused a breakdown in communications. Dr Hartfield was encouraged to consider an application which would enable WGH Ilesha to upgrade all round and meet the new standards for nursing training.

Submitting a proposal for Joint Funding

In January 1968 I returned from leave and set about fulfilling all the requirements of ICCO's 'model application'. This involved a careful plan in three phases, area maps, site plans, architect's drawings for all the buildings envisaged, with provisional estimates, and then necessary authorisations from the Hospital Management Committee, Methodist Church Nigeria, Methodist Missionary Society London, and the formal approval from the Ministries of Health, and of Economic Planning for the Western State, and the Federal Ministry of Economic Development for the whole country. A Methodist architect called John G L Poulson, from Pontefract, UK, whom I had met while on leave, offered to do the Nursing School plans for us without charge, as part of his strategy for opening a branch of his architect's firm in Nigeria. He did very well for us then, and we owe him nothing but gratitude. The troubles he had later are now behind him.

Liaison was maintained with the Nederlands ambassador in Lagos who was always most helpful, Dr S L Adesuyi at the Federal Ministry of Health, and of course, with the local community. The complexity of the operation and all the detail required did make one wonder how any local agency with less expertise on the ground than we had at Ilesha had any chance of obtaining a grant. For the 'joint funding ' part we submitted the cost of buildings already completed with help from the Nigerian government, the Jephcott Trust and from our own WGH resources, about £40,000 out of £160,000. (The Nigerian pound was then valued at 1.25 to the pound sterling. How different from the present plight of the Nigerian currency at about 125 nairas to the £1!) By November the document and all attachments were ready. The Nursing Council of Nigeria inspected again, saw the new nurses' hostel and modern children's wards, and the plans for further development. They agreed that the hospital could be upgraded for SRN, provided that the other improved facilities could be in place within the next three years.

Fig 6.1 *The Development plan, 1963 and 1975*

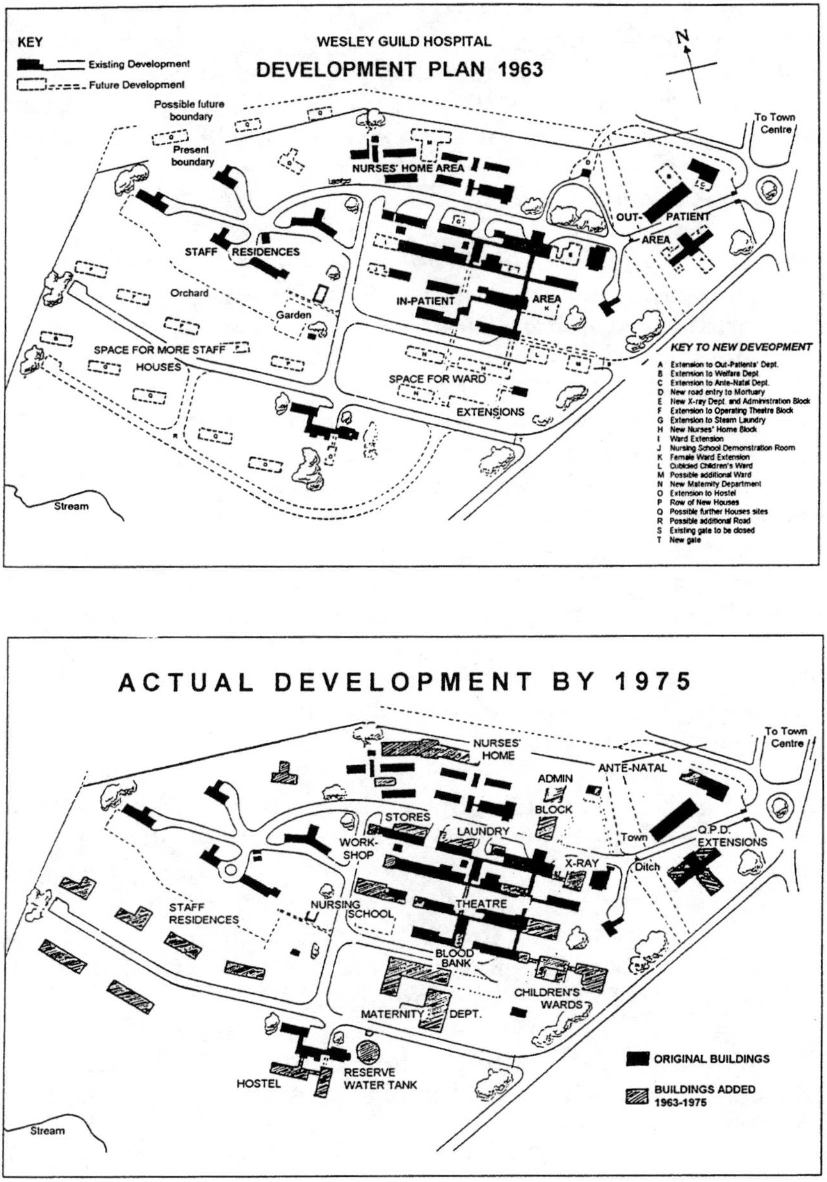

Students who entered as from January 1968 would be eligible to sit the new examinations. With a great sense of relief the application packet was dispatched to ICCO in Utrecht, Holland. The documents were worked on further by the agency in order to satisfy the requirements of the Nederlands Foreign Affairs office. More documentation was sent as requested, and the telegram of approval from Holland did not arrive in Ilesha till October 1969. I was on leave at that time and had to travel to The Hague to sign the Co-financing Agreement on behalf of the hospital. What a saga it had been!

Using the grant to complete our 'Development Plan'

The first grant arrived in February 1970. Buildings proceeded apace, beginning with the nursing school, new female ward, utilities building, nurses' home shower block and a staff residence. The official opening of the Nursing School was on July 4th, with the Dutch ambassador, Mr Arnout de Waal, present and Mrs Kofoworola Pratt, the most eminent nurse in Nigeria and President of the Nursing Council. The occasion was combined with Graduation Day for those just qualified and Mrs Pratt gave out the certificates and pinned on the much-prized Wesley Guild badges. It was also the launch of the Nurses League to unite all Wesley Guild nurses past and present, and the first Saturday in July has remained their regular time for meeting each year ever since.

The plans of several major buildings remained to be finalised. These included the Administration Block, the site chosen for which was not far from the hospital Mortuary. At times the police brought us the bodies of beggars (classified as 'paupers') for whom no relatives could be traced, leaving the bodies unclaimed. In the tropical heat, within three or four days the odour from such bodies could be unpleasant, to say the least. If the police did not act, the doctors sometimes had to recruit some labour staff, and drive the hospital lorry themselves with the body and team of helpers out to the 'Strangers' Cemetery' on the edge of town where the body could be buried. Adding a Refrigerated Mortuary extension was therefore seen as essential.

The biggest building in the whole scheme was the new Maternity Department. In conformity with the Morling 'Development Plan' this was to be on a new site below the other wards, an area previously used informally as a football pitch. The old Maternity Ward would be released for other purposes; and as things turned out part went for use by the Central

Fig 6.2 *Gateway to the hospital as it was in 1974*

Fig 6.3 *Stella Liony Memorial Chapel, with the Admission Room and Male Ward beyond*

Pharmacy and part for a Psychiatric Ward. The New Maternity was going to be an entirely fresh start, and allow for original thinking. Dr Hartfield, who had been our obstetrician since he returned to Ilesha with his MRCOG in January 1966, drew the first plans in very simple outline form in June 1969. However, the following month he was transferred by the Methodist Church to work at Ituk Mbang Hospital in the east. This was the other major Methodist medical institution in Nigeria, and it had been released from the southern part of Biafra as the Federal army moved in from the coast and northward towards the Ibo heartland. So much needed doing in its rehabilitation and Jonathon stayed nine months. Dr Horsfall came to Ilesha from UCH Ibadan Obs/Gynae Department to do a very useful six months locum. When Jonathon returned in April 1970, we had to bring in Design Group Ibadan as architects, as John Poulson could no longer help. The plans produced for a 72-bed unit looked lovely on paper but when costed proved far to expensive, £90,000 not £50,000 as originally estimated. Though the Dutch authorities did increase their grant to allow for inflation, the maternity plans had to be scaled down from seventy-two beds to forty. Two L-shaped wings on either side of a central delivery unit had to be re-thought. The easiest way was to leave the delivery unit but excise one wing, leaving space for the other to built at a later date if resources and demand made that possible and necessary. In fact it never has been built, though a philanthropic club in Ilesha, 'The Social Elites', did adopt it as a project for one day in the future.

Mr John Mellanby, who had been retained as consultant engineer for six months from November 1969, wisely suggested that the enlarged hospital would probably consume 50% more water, and provision for a better reserve supply should be made. We were just in time to have a 100,000 gallon circular low-level tank included in the scheme, and this was one of the last items to be completed. However, from about this time on, water in the mains supply became so chronically short the tank never filled up. Ilesha town had begun to outgrow its supply through increasing population, and wider use of water-borne sanitation.

Completion in time for the Sixtieth Jubilee

Building went on through 1971 and was finally completed in 1972. In September of that year the Sixtieth Jubilee of the Methodist medical work in Nigeria (1912–1972) was celebrated with the official opening of the Administration Block by Mr H S A Adedeji (an Ilesha man who

Fig 6.4 *Official opening of the new Maternity Department in 1972, the hospital's Sixtieth Jubilee, by His Highness the Owa-Obokun of Ijeshaland*

Fig 6.5 *Front of the new Maternity Department*

was Permanent Secretary of the Ministry of Finance). In addition the new Maternity Block was opened by the Commissioner for Health, Ibadan, in the presence of a Dutch government representative to whom warm thanks was given. Over 100 mothers were delivered in the first two months, and all were appreciative of the better facilities offered without any increase in fees. The doctors using the Department found it was a joy to work in, it was so functionally well designed. With reason it could be claimed to be the best maternity department in Nigeria.

The hospital, now with nearly 200 beds (197 to be precise), was as fully developed as the site would allow. The size of the hospital staff, and the work being done, reached a peak, which was to drop off a little in the next two or three years, mainly because of economic restrictions. In 1972 there were seven doctors and about seventy qualified nurses and midwives of all grades, ten other senior staff (in pharmacy, laboratory, X-ray, administration, maintenance, catering and a chaplain), forty-five clerical and technical staff, and about 100 artisans, maids and labour staff. The amount of medical care being given was prodigious. The 1972 statistics show, in round figures:

In-patients - nearly 7,000 in the year,
Out-patient attendances, nearly 300,000 (about 1000 a day),
Deliveries - nearly 1000 in the year,
Operations, major and minor - 5000.

In the seven out-stations in the district, eleven midwives recorded another 200,000 attendances and 500 deliveries.

The nursing school in its new building had, for the first time, a Nigerian Principal Tutor, Mr Lawrence Olu Babajide. The were two other nurse-tutors and 140 student nurses or pupil midwives, and they were working to the 'New Standards of Training'. The hospital and school did indeed have much to be thankful for.

CHAPTER 7

CHRISTIAN MISSION – INTRINSIC TO IT ALL

While on leave I was sometimes asked, 'How did you divide your time between the medical work and the missionary work?' My answer was, 'We didn't.' Both went together. We were part of the local church. We shared our skills. The medical work was one means of demonstrating the love of God in practice. The hospital's ministry of healing, together with preaching and teaching, were all key elements in the church's mission. However, the story from 1952 has been mainly about the medical side, the people, the buildings, the finance, the training programmes, and the patients around which all this activity turned. A similar story might have been written about any medical institution, its struggles and set-backs and its successes and achievements. There is a 'church side' which remains to be given more fully, and that relates to WGH staff and their role within the Methodist Church of Nigeria and the wider community of the country, and the continued links with the Methodist Church and Wesley Guilds in Britain.

Missionaries as members of the local church

When my wife and I arrived in Ilesha in 1952 we were soon made aware of the flourishing local church, with congregations of 600 in the mornings and 200 in the evenings, fearless preaching and sacrificial giving, at least for special occasions such as the 'Harvest offering' where every man had to produce 30/- and every woman 12/6d. The missionaries were there as lay members like others in the congregation, and expected to attend the one English-speaking class meeting, and pay their dues. In no sense were we there as the pioneer missionaries of earlier years, surrounded, as they would have put it, by 'pagan darkness'. There were still powerful traditional priests, fears of witchcraft and 'ju-ju', and cultural practices with which the church had to contend. It was now the local church which was in charge. Our work in the hospital helped Christians greatly in their every day confrontation with the many challenges they were up against. Some of the missionaries were recognized as Methodist Local Preachers, and were given appointments to preach on the Plan, usually at the monthly English service at Otapete church in the town, but occasionally in villages with an interpreter. Dr Mulligan was the only one who learned sufficient Yoruba to conduct a service and preach on his own. In this the pioneer missionaries were far ahead of us.

Opportunities in the hospital

Within the hospital, there were regular ward services, but no aggressive evangelism or counting of heads. The senior staff had their prayer assembly at 7.00 to 7.15 am, the beginning of the working day, and the nurses an evening prayer time too. Once we had the Stella Liony Memorial Chapel on the new site, it became the custom for Monday, Wednesday, Friday prayers to be in English, led by doctors, week and week about. Tuesday, Thursday and Saturday prayers were in Yoruba, and were led by the Chaplain, when we had one, or by Mr Awodiya faithfully throughout all his years in the hospital - a remarkable record.

On Wednesday evenings the resident staff, missionaries and Nigerian senior staff as they joined us, had a fellowship in one of the houses for discussion and prayer. Every fourth Wednesday it was a full Staff Committee in the office. In our fellowship we found we had a great variety of approaches to our faith, such as Osmund Mulligan with his Northern Irish background, very traditional and strongly Bible-based, and Jonathon Hartfield, delightfully free-thinking and liberal, but genuinely concerned for the truth; yet all of us united through our common life together. This was so important in making the hospital a happy community where we could all give our best to the patients.

Harvest with a difference

Harvest festivals are enjoyed in Nigeria as much as anywhere. I recalled the 1970 harvest in our Christmas letter home.

> 'The decorations to the Hospital Chapel were much as usual with yellow canna lillies, white jasmine, pink beaugainvillea, red ixora, arches of palm leaves, fruit and vegetables of all kinds, and whole banana trees on either side of the pulpit reaching up to the roof. You could just about see where the preacher should be! The service however was different. We wanted the thanksgiving to be real and

relevant for our hospital community, so it had been announced a few days beforehand that representatives from the various departments would be invited up to the front to voice their thanks for special blessings in the past year, and to bring some symbol or offering. They came, and a fascinating procession it proved to be, each saying their piece, then standing aside as the hospital drummers banged out a native rhythm between each contribution. The laboratory technicians came first to thank God for their new blood bank which had been opened the week before by the Military Governor, and placed two pints of blood on the communion table. Nursing students followed with a new box of chalks and a blackboard duster to say thank-you for their lovely new Nursing School opened in August by the head of the Nursing Council of Nigeria. Male Ward nurses expressed thanks for their new sanitary annexe and brought toilet rolls as a very practical symbol! The midwives came with a roll of architect's plans for the hoped-for new Maternity Department due to be built the coming year. One-armed Matthew from Welfare Department brought his thank-offering and mentioned especially Margaret Woodland's help in improving the Immunisation Department. A Children's Ward nurse came up with a tin of milk, and a little child in her arms that had recovered from kwashiorkor, and an Ibo nurse most movingly thanked God for the survival of herself, and all her family, through the civil war while she was in 'Biafra', and for her immediate re-acceptance back at Ilesha, together with ten others, for completion of nurse training. She presented five guineas for the Samaritan Fund. Michael Stephen, accounts clerk, thanked God we had been able to keep the hospital accounts straight despite a gap of nine months between Mr Pope leaving and a new accountant coming. Then Dr Osmund Mulligan, the surgeon, brought up Dr Daniel Laosebikan, who had just arrived the previous day to be Surgical Registrar, and in the name of all the medical staff gave heartfelt thanks for (what we hoped would be) our first permanent staff Nigerian doctor. Finally Rev D.B. Esan, our beloved Chairman of the District, and Chairman of the HMC for so many years, brought all our thanks together in a closing prayer. The Spirit had indeed been with us.'

Student Christian Movement, and the Nurses' Choir

From 1953 my wife began organizing a Student Christian Movement branch for the nurses, which linked up with other SCM branches in nearby secondary schools. It was strong throughout the Western Region and helped many to an intelligent commitment. During 1946–1948 in UK, while still Jean Frost, she had been an SCM Travelling Secretary, and now in Nigeria enjoyed this continued involvement with students. She also trained a Nurses' Choir which achieved remarkably high standards, and, to this day, she misses the opportunity to prepare for an Annual Carol Service each Christmas. Sometimes doctors and senior Nigerian male staff were brought in to sing bass or tenor. Syncopated Yoruba lyrics were popular, but we did not make use of native drumming talent as much as the church does now to such good effect.

Chaplains to care for staff and patients

It was in 1957 that the Methodist Church first put 'Wesley Guild Hospital, Ilesha' onto its List of Stations, and the first Chaplain to be appointed was Pastor E O Osinguwa. He did his best to serve both staff and patients, made good use of the Methodist Book Van when on tour from Shagamu, and in Easter 1959 helped organize a special series of meetings led by the Rev. John Crossley, a Methodist from Ibadan. John was more fluent at preaching in Yoruba than most Yorubas, and the study he had made of the Christian approach to Islam gave his message a balanced, yet greatly effective appeal.

The Rev. Abraham Idowu came in 1962, and was the first ordained minister to be Chaplain. Most who followed him stayed 2 years, some doing better than others. Many found it difficult not having a fixed congregation (apart from the staff) who came to them, rather than having themselves to go out to a 'congregation' of patients changing every few days. Abraham, in fact, adapted well, and found patients eager to attach themselves to a church, whether Methodist, or Anglican or whatever, after their time in hospital. In 1968 the chaplain was the Rev. Moses Osinuga and he started a special service for patients due for discharge that day. One night that year he found himself ministering to a great crowd of relatives and patients admitted after a major lorry accident. Several people had died, many had injuries, all were shocked and confused. The irony was that they were all members of the Cherubim and Seraphim, an indigenous church which normally will have nothing to do with hospitals and medical care, believing only in holy water and prayer. Moses diverted most of the milling crowd of hangers on into the Chapel nearby to rest - and to give the medical staff space to work. He later reported,

> 'The situation, though a tragic one, yet presented an opportunity for bringing the Gospel, with its message of the love, mercy and Almightiness of God to the sympathising crowd. Such a door of opportunity to witness for Him in times of pain, and in times of joy, continues to be open to us.'

There were often times when we felt quite useless. On one occasion a business man travelling into Ilesha had noticed a mentally-damaged woman dressed in rags begging at the roadside with a large ulcer on her leg. He took pity on her, carried her in his own car to a medicine seller who cleaned and covered the sore with a bandage. Then he bought her a new blouse and wrapper, and brought her to the hospital for continued care, leaving a small deposit for her costs, just like the Good Samaritan. We admitted her to a side-ward because of her mental state, and the smelly sore. This was soon greatly improved, but mentally she was lonely, we could not get through to her. She hid behind the ward door. The hospital environment was too strange. Eventually we decided she would be happier out on the roadside. We took her back, hoping people would still give her alms, but felt guilty ourselves that we had no real answer to her long-term need. Dr Cannon had a consoling thought.

> 'It was all very well for the Good Samaritan,' he said, ' but what about the inn-keeper?'

It was to be thirty years before that long-term answer was to be found through the work of Ros Colwill (see page 143).

Cooperation in theological training
From 1961 courses were arranged at WGH for those being trained for the Ministry of both Methodist and Anglican churches at Immanuel College, Ibadan. About 15 ordinands would stay for a week to study 'The Christian Approach to Healing', with tutorials from doctors, nurses and Christian ministers and Muslim leaders. The 1968 course covered such subjects as:

'Functions of a Christian hospital' — Medical Superintendent

'Hospital organization and etiquette' — The Matron

'A Christian's attitude to juju, witchcraft and demon possession' — Pastor Elton, an Apostolic pastor from Ilesha town - a good friend of the hospital

'A Christian doctrine of healing'

'Muslim attitudes to disease and healing',

'Family planning', 'Women's problems', 'Child health'

'How to help the dying'

'Hospital chaplaincy - what it is'.

The courses were sometimes extended to Salvation Army cadets, and were always appreciated. They continued until 1972 and must have contributed to a better appreciation of the Christian understanding of disease and healing, though it was at a time when sects offering 'miracle healing' were on the increase.

Healing the spirit

Christians in Nigeria live in a culture where fears are very real, and one must have a whole-person approach to illness. The missionary outpost at Afon, across the border into the Northern Region south of Ilorin, was remote. A small bible school was being run there by a missionary - Kathleen Ormrod at that time - and her assistant . One student had an attack of acute mania while there and was taken to Ilorin hospital, but died. The smallpox God, Shopona was believed by the villagers to have caused it. Shopona was said to be able to cause 'black small-pox' which produced no rash, but mania instead. The following term another lad was put in the same room. He was a Christian, and knew the story but did not believe it - until he went mad too. Kathleen brought him to Ilesha, and we nursed him in a side ward. He was certainly psychotically disturbed. We examined him physically and found he also had an ear discharge following acute otitis media, so he had been having severe earache. We also discovered from the Kathleen that he had been blamed for taking the water-bucket of a fellow student for himself. That water had been carried a mile. He felt guilty. And finally there were doubtless repressed fears from the Shopona story which he had been told.

Fig 7.1 *Pastor Sydney and Cis Elton*

To cure him required penicillin to treat the ear, counselling to help him face his guilt over the water and decide how to make it up to his fellow student, and sympathetic prayer to overcome his fears. For the latter we asked our friend Pastor Elton to help, since he understood the demonic forces in local culture so well. The young man made a good recovery.

This broad understanding of healing was spread more widely throughout Methodist churches in Nigeria by the observance of a Hospital Sunday in July each year. One of my tasks as Medical Secretary for the Methodist Church was to send out suggestions for the worship on that day, readings, prayers, and even a sermon text and three points to preach on! How often they were used, I do not know. Anglican churches had a similar day at St Luke's Tide in October. In 1966 I was booked to preach for this service at the Anglican All Saints Church in the city Ibadan, seventy-five miles from Ilesha. It was at a time when all the Western State mission hospitals were in something of a dispute with the Ministry of Health, partly due to very difficult Permanent Secretary. My prepared sermon included material about the great contribution being made to health by all the mission hospitals, and calling on the churches and the whole community for their support. To my surprise, as I entered the pulpit, I found the entire leadership of the Ministry of Health in the front pew, including the said Permanent Secretary who was to read the first lesson! I did not change the sermon.

Methodist Church Nigeria medical work

Working for the church at national level

Because of the leading position of WGH in Nigerian Methodism, the doctor in charge generally found himself as Secretary for the church's Medical Committee, with responsibility for keeping an eye on all the church's medical services in the Western and Eastern Regions. The latter included Ituk Mbang Hospital, Amachara Hospital and Bethesda Hospital Ikachi, and also serving on the Board of the new united training centre, Queen Elizabeth Hospital, which was being built at Umuahia. This was a joint venture with the Presbyterian and Anglican Churches to provide a base for training all nursing and technical staff, though not doctors. In 1960 I attended an Assembly of the Christian Council of Nigeria as a Methodist delegate. It was in Abeokuta, and the king, the Alake of Abeokuta, was receiving guests and representatives from every corner of Nigeria. He was a man of great dignity, and every inch the Christian gentleman. The lovely story was told that many years ago he asked one of our missionaries to design a chapel for his wives. 'They are all Methodists,' he added. 'What seating accommodation will the chapel require?' asked the missionary. 'Oh, about three hundred,' came the reply!

Church autonomy, and help to Cote d'Ivoire

In 1962 the Methodist Church Nigeria became autonomous from its parent church in Britain, with its own Conference, and from being Synod Medical Secretary for the Western District I became Conference Medical Secretary, covering west and east. Part of the task was to keep in touch with Wesley Guild movement in Britain and this was done through written 'Newsflash' items, a film-strip 'Ilesha Today', colour slides, taped messages and a 40-minutes film, 'Road to Dabou'. This was prepared for the centenary of Methodist medical work in 1964 and the special project of building a new hospital in Cote d'Ivoire (Ivory Coast) at Dabou. For this the film unit came first to Ilesha to show scenes of Ilesha Wesley Guild Hospital in action, then switched to Ivory Coast to show the needs waiting to be met there. Many building ideas were in fact borrowed from Ilesha, and the first doctor in charge at Dabou was Dr Paul Snell who had spent an 'elective' period at Ilesha as a medical student. Marion Lethbridge moved from Ilesha to Dabou in 1965 to be the first Matron. For my wife and me it was interesting to be involved in the Centenary project because the 100 years pointed back to 1864 when the 'Hospital of Universal Love' had been started in Hankow, China, where we ourselves had begun our missionary career.

Ecumenical work

Christian Council of Nigeria
As a Methodist representative I also found myself working within the Christian Council of Nigeria, and then appointed Secretary of the CCN Medical Board in 1960 when Dr Theo Mess, of Wusasa Hospital, Zaria, retired to go home.. This put me in touch with the medical work of most of the Protestant Christian missions in the country. In 1963 Jean and I had a visit from Dr G A Ademola, and his wife Rosa, on their way from Lagos to the Iyi-Enu Anglican Hospital, Onitsha in the east. They were talking then about some kind of Christian Medical Fellowship to unite all Christian doctors. In 1968, now as the Medical Adviser to the Federal Government he helped start a *Nigerian Voluntary Agencies Medical Services Committee (NVAMSC)* which brought together the CCN Medical Board, the Catholic Medical Secretariat and the Northern Missions Medical Advisory Council. The door was left open for any Muslim voluntary agency to join as well, but none appeared to exist in Nigeria. The intention was good, but it was during the civil war and developments were hampered. CCN Assemblies did not take place during those years, 1966–1969, and, in any case, no one could ever remember what the letters NVAMSC stood for!

Christian Health Association of Nigeria
In February 1970, shortly after the war was over, Nigeria was visited by Dr James C. McGilvray, Director of the Christian Medical Commission (CMC) of the World Council of Churches in Geneva, together with a strong team, Tracey Jones from America, Dr Theo Mess (of the Church Missionary Society - back again) and Dr John Wilkinson (Church of Scotland, over from Kenya). Since 1965 Dr McGilvray had been fostering the development of national Christian health consultative bodies in Africa and Asia, beginning with the Private Hospital Association of Malawi By 1968 over 20 such associations were in existence, and the initiative led in turn to the formation of the CMC in Geneva. With the end of the Biafran war the CMC wanted to see what were the possibilities

for enhanced cooperation between the churches doing medical work in Nigeria. Unfortunately there was some breakdown in communication. No one was there to meet the visitors at the airport or had prepared anything except for a booking at Mainland Hotel. They were surprised not to find a large assembly gathered to hear them, and nearly turned round and went straight back to Switzerland, such was their disappointment. However, Dr Ademola was there and I did get to Lagos myself, as did one or two others. Discussions were useful. Confidence was a little restored. The situation was really put back on course when Sir Louis Mbanefo, a great Ibo Christian leader no longer limited to the bounds of 'Biafra', was able to visit Geneva and confirm that Nigeria was ready to go ahead.

The NVAMSC resumed meeting occasionally, but the real break-through came at a national conference in December 1973 in Ibadan, when it was decided that, since no Muslim agency had appeared, the name should be changed to Christian Health Association of Nigeria (CHAN). The acronym could be spoken easily, and it caught on. The first full-time National Secretary, found for us by Dr McGilvray, and with support from the Church Missionary Society, Dr Stanley Lang, came to live at WGH Ilesha in July 1974. The ecumenical cooperation on health work within CHAN proved a vital source of strength, especially in providing a united voice in its dealings with State Ministries of Health. CHAN was later to develop an agency pattern, beginning with a body to import and manufacture pharmaceuticals at the cheapest possible price for all the church-related member hospitals. I went with the CHAN team to Geneva to help negotiate the start-up grants of what came to be known as 'CHANPHARM'. It has been such a boon to church hospitals and health services as the economic situation has worsened. Later, CHAN Primary Care was to become an equally important agency for all church-related health work in the country.

The Wesley Guilds

The link remained unbroken

At various points through the story so far the Guilds in Britain and Nigeria have come in for mention. Links with the church in Britain, and the Wesley Guild movement in particular, were maintained through letters, tapes and photographs, and through direct contacts and the taking of meetings by the missionaries when they were on leave. In the course of their 'deputation work', they went the rounds of the churches, chapels and Guilds, to tell them what we had been doing. Enthusiasm was often overwhelming. The challenge to raise money for the rebuilding in 1953 heightened interest, and the first carved Guild badge sent by Guild Holiday Homes remained over the arch of the main hospital gateway. In 1956 a second carved Guild badge was ordered for the Nurses' Home at the hospital on the strength of money raised in her home town of Portessie by Gwladys Stewart, who as Sister Charlesworth had been the first nurse to come to Ilesha in 1917. She was still as active as ever. In March 1957, before the plaque left Britain, it was placed on the platform and dedicated at a great London Rally in Westminster Central Hall with 2,700 Guilders present, such was the support in those days.

As we reached the 1970s regular news from Ilesha was being sent to the Guilds through the MMS Youth Secretary. Guild support for medical students going to Ilesha for their 'elective' study period was particularly welcome. At least two were to return as medical missionaries themselves after qualification.

CHAPTER 8

LIGHT AND SHADE

During all this period of expansion to meet the requirements of nurse training, much else was happening for which we were very thankful. There was good news and plenty of it, but there was also bad. Clouds were gathering on the horizon which foreshadowed an uncertain future. First the good news.

Medical staffing

Doctors from many countries

As the doctor in charge I had to be constantly on the look-out for doctors and other staff, and it was surprising from where the offers came. One unusual appointment was that of Dr Makoto Miyazaki who came to us from Japan in June 1968, with his wife (also a doctor) and their two children. Makoto was a surgeon, and Fellow of the Japanese Association of Urologists. He was sponsored by a Unitarian group in Japan, and supported by the Japanese Christian Medical Association who looked on him and his wife as their missionaries to the people of Nigeria. During their two year tour they brought a new dimension to our international fellowship. Japanese abroad were not so common then as they are now.

Dr Miyazaki's presence enabled Dr Mulligan in September 1968 to have another two months of language study. It also gave him time to expand a system of diagnostic punch-cards, previously used only in the maternity department, to cover all patients over five years. For this he obtained another WACMR research grant. These cards had a series of holes round the edge, which could be punched open, and then sorted using a knitting needle. Every patient had a card on discharge filled in with the final diagnosis and essential details. It was time consuming but did facilitate research. Nowadays computerised records do it so much better!

Dr Betty Abraham, from South India, came in June 1970 as the Miyazakis left, and first kept the Paediatric department together till Mary Thwaites arrived in October. She then moved to Medicine to help me, and finally to Obstetrics when Dr Hartfield left in April 1971. In a hospital like Ilesha this kind of multi-competent generalist doctor was what we needed, and Betty coped with all sides with charm and skill.

Dr Stephen Mathai came to us from India a little later for two years (1973–1975). He was a graduate of the well-known Christian Medical College of Vellore, competent, quiet-spoken and adaptable. He spent a year each in surgery and paediatrics, as needs arose.

It was my duty as Medical Superintendent to ensure that an all round service was maintained, and to encourage doctors not to be rigidly limited to one speciality. For myself it involved filling gaps in the various specialities as doctors came and went, acting as surgeon, obstetrician or paediatrician as the need arose, but accepting one's limitations. Only when staffing was at full strength could I keep my permanent lines in Medicine and hospital administration. The experience was invaluable, and from it came the concept of 'tropical general practice', which I was to develop during the years 1975–1985.

Three more missionary doctors came in the 1973 to 1975 period. Dr Jenny Mee, paediatrician, who came from Britain, was of Hong Kong Chinese extraction. Dr Arun and Christine Baksi had recently married and both came to work full time. Arun was an Indian and a specialist physician, and Chris, from Liverpool, an obstetrician. Both were lovely people, and fascinating characters, keen to help in any way possible. Chris's father had been the commissionaire at the entrance to the headquarters of the Methodist Missionary Society at 25 Marylebone Road, London, and it had always been her ambition to come overseas one day herself.

Doctors for short periods

Many doctors came for a few months or a year and it is impossible to profile all in detail. They included Norman James, from the United States, John Patrick (who went on to work at Segwema Hospital in Sierra Leone, Hazel Wilson (of the Society of Friends), Michael and Judith Steel (both gold medallists in their medical school; Michael's brother was to become Sir David Steel, the Liberal politician), Hugh Edwards and John Bourne, all from Britain; Dr Anne Bosma from Holland, and another doctor from India, K C Mathai who came for four months. Dr Horsfall and Dr Robinson moved over to help us as locums from UCH Ibadan, and we had a few senior Nigerian doctors who joined us for short periods, Dr J M Falaiye, physician (1966) and Dr Yemi Babatunde, obstetrician (1972).

The need for more Nigerian doctors
Pre-registration doctors came in regular succession following the lead of Dr J.B. Familusi and Dr S A Olowe. Dr Sam Oloruntoba, who came in 1967, later developed the Olaolu Hospital in Ilorin with a group of Christian general practitioners. The reputation of the centre was high. The State Governor was among its patients. The hospital has a Christmas custom of celebrating 'Carols on the Rocks' on a flood-lit natural rock platform near the hospital entrance. Sam plays the organ, the nurses' choir sings, and Christian leaders share in the service. Over 3000 people from that predominantly Muslim town turn up each year. Sam says it was the nurses' carol service at WGH Ilesha which gave him the idea.

Many other doctors came too, did their six to twelve months housemanship, and went on to make their particular contributions in various branches of the health service. Among them were Dr Itam, Dr Bisi Oke, Dr Kabba Joiner (a Gambian), Dr Adebajo, Dr Thorpe, Dr Bode Akintade, Dr Ebiekpi and Dr Dominic. The latter two had been put through medical school with scholarships from the Methodist Church Nigeria. We enjoyed having them all, and also greatly appreciated the two surgical registrars, Dr Laosebikan and Dr Duvie. They learned much while at Ilesha, and all have given much in service since, but none applied to stay on for a permanent appointment. Some wanted to pursue speciality courses for their life-time career, which meant moving to a teaching hospital in Nigeria or overseas. Some, like Dr Oloruntoba, went into private practice with the hope of greater clinical freedom, and reasonable financial security.

Recruiting doctors for a career at WGH Ilesha proved to be difficult. The going rate-for-the-job set by the Nigerian government was always offered, even though it meant paying two or three times what the missionaries received, but the financial incentive was insufficient. In April 1972 we tried a new style of advertisement:

> 'Outstanding opportunity for an Obstetrician/Gynaecologist, qualified MRCOG who, because of his Christian conviction wants to do more than just make a comfortable living'.

It caused some press comment, but produced only one enquirer, and he eventually said no, feeling that to work at a hospital like Ilesha was 'eccentric'. 'A Nigerian cannot be a missionary in his own country'. WGH Ilesha did not fit in to the normal career ladder. In this matter we had to admit failure. It was a problem to which we were to return.

Nurses, administrators and technical staff

Matrons, Sisters and Tutors

On the nursing side WGH was much more successful in attracting senior Nigerians as nursing sisters. Marion Lethbridge took on the nursing leadership, becoming Matron in succession to Elsie Ludlow in 1960. She continued till December 1965, her winsome manner earning her the love and respect of all the staff. She in turn handed on to Miss A.A. Abiodun, our first Nigerian for the job, and already highly experienced before coming to Ilesha. By that time we also had two Nigerian Sisters, Mrs Rebecca Komolafe (the first to be so promoted) and Mrs Dorothy Ogedengbe, who was from British Guyana in the Caribbean. She had met and married her Nigerian lawyer husband, Mr Samuel Ogedengbe, while both were studying in London and staying in Methodist International House. In addition there were two Nigerian Assistant Nursing Superintendents as well as the four missionary Sisters. In 1970 the HMC used its prerogative and selected one of the missionaries, Sister Doreen Habbershaw, to succeed Miss Abiodun, although by that time there were 10 Nigerian Sisters. She was deemed best for the job and amply fulfilled expectations till the handover to Mrs Komolafe in 1975. Dorothy's turn came later.

The Nursing School story was similar. Enid Blake left in 1958, and Marion Lethbridge filled in for two years as Tutor until the arrival of Margaret Gardner. She was the one to see the School through its transformation to fulfil the new standards, and showed great skill in matching the teaching equipment in the school with what was actually in use on the wards. For example, the trolley used on the wards for dispensing medicines to the patients at the bed-side, was replicated in the school. The set-up of trays used for minor procedures was precisely the same. The student nurse coming for practical experience on the wards was immediately on familiar ground. In conformity with new nomenclature Margaret became the first *Principal Tutor,* and was the one to hand on to Mr Lawrence Babajide when he returned from further training in UK to take on the responsibility in March 1972. When Lawrence's application through the Methodist Church in Britain first arrived at Ilesha, the comment was made that his qualifications and experience, as listed on his curriculum vitae, 'seemed almost too good to be true'. He was to prove fully competent, but the appointment was not be without its problems in the tense times that were to come later.

Administrative staff

Mr Hezekiah Awodiya moved up from being Assistant Hospital Manager to full Manager in 1958, and continued as such until 1976, a few months after the hospital takeover. His faithful, honest service for so long was a steady rock on which a corruption-free Nigerian staff was built. Not everyone realised how much was owed to him. By 1964 he headed a growing team of 20 clerks, cashiers, records staff and clerical assistants, and 40 maintenance and labour staff. By 1974 the numbers were 26 clerical and 65 labour staff, and in addition there were 35 maids and kitchen staff who were responsible to the Matron.

In 1965 Mr Jonathan Pope joined the staff from MMS as the first qualified Accountant, and how glad we were to have him. He was well trained and experienced through working in the Greater London Council, and thought Ilesha's accounts were a mere trifle in comparison. Perhaps like many accountants, he was a pessimist at heart and was never happier than when we were up against it. The financial crisis through which the hospital went in 1966–1967 was no problem to him.

Laboratory staff

The diagnostic laboratory at Ilesha under Mr Lawrence Beyer was acknowledged to be one of the best in the country, apart from those in the big teaching hospitals. Lawrence came in 1965 and combined a love of organ playing with a remarkable ability to organize space. Within a very small area every laboratory 'department' had its own bench - haematology, bacteriology, histology etc, and there was an efficient blood transfusion service besides. In 1970 one of Lawrence's trainees,

Fig 8.1 *Miss Ade Abiodun, first Nigerian Matron, as from December 1965, together with Sister Doreen Habbershaw who became Matron in 1970*

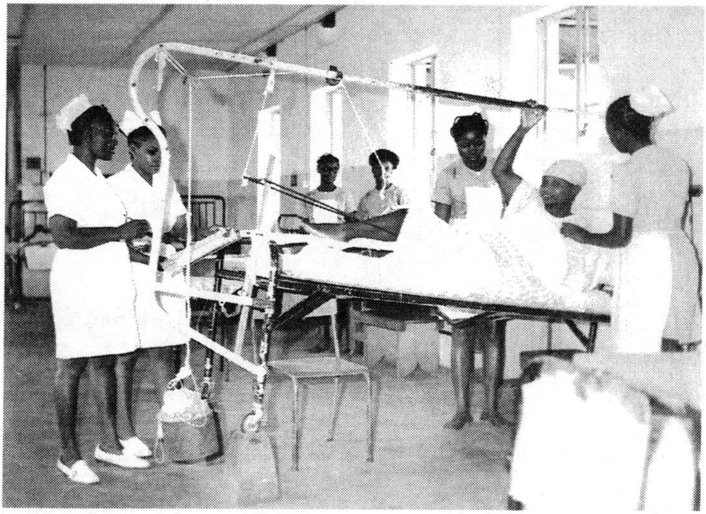

Fig 8.2 *Mrs Rebecca Komolafe, and Mrs Dorothy Ogedengbe on their Sisters' rounds in the Female Ward*

Mr Theophilus Olawoye, was successful at first attempt for the Intermediate examination of the Institute of Medical Laboratory Technology (London) and went on to get his finals in Edinburgh, before returning to Ilesha in 1974 to take charge. From September 1970 Ilesha was recognized for training for the Nigerian Institute of Laboratory Technology, and seven students were enrolled. The success rate was good and some went on from Part 1 to do Part 2 at larger centres. It all seemed a long way from the simple beginnings with Mr James Balogun at the old hospital. James stayed for 34 years and retired in 1971, latterly looking after the out-patient laboratory. Mr Amos Ajayi, who came back with his UK training in 1964 did not stay long, and Mr Sam Akpaete, though without the higher diploma, gave excellent service in his place and stayed on till 1975. Many others also joined the laboratory team.

Pharmacists

In the pharmacy, Miss Kathleen Owen served for five years, and began the training of dispensing assistants. Miss Joan Stephenson took over from her in July 1964, having come to Ilesha from UCH Ibadan intending to stay for a year. She stayed for nine years(!), formalised the training for those now called pharmacy assistants, and also introduced annual tendering from local companies and bulk buying for 80% of the drugs used in the hospital. Since she got wholesale prices the drug bill was substantially reduced, and there was seldom any item not available from stock. In October 1973 Mr Steve Athey arrived to take on the job, and was joined two months later by our first Nigerian pharmacist, Mr Akin Oni. They were in time to utilise a Jephcott Trust grant to equip and organize the new central pharmacy and manufacturing section in the part of the old maternity ward allocated to them.

Radiographers

The X-ray Department, processing over 2500 films a year, was looked after by Michael Abe alone till 1970, when he left for a job in Owo. Other radiography assistants took his place, and Professor Bohrer of UCH Ibadan helped greatly as Visiting Radiologist, conducting fortnightly teaching sessions with the doctors on the interesting or puzzling films that had been taken.

The looming financial crisis

More staff needed, and then higher salaries

Our very success on so many sides was also becoming a liability. Clouds were gathering. Once the children's wards extensions were completed in 1969, and hospital beds increased from 142 to 160 there was an obvious need for more nurses. In addition the new standards of nurse training to which we were committed required an improved ratio of nurses per patient-bed. 1969–1970 estimates were submitted allowing for inflation (10% at that time) plus extra for an increased establishment, £20,000 on top of £121,000. On advice from the Nursing School, nursing sister posts were doubled, and staff-nurse midwife posts increased by 50%. Ways of raising the extra revenue had to be found before this could be approved. The prospects looked even more daunting when a government commission for revision of civil service salaries, headed by a Mr Elwood, published its report in May 1969. This recommended a 90% increase of salaries for nurses. The hospital was committed to paying the 'rate for the job' as decided by government, but how on earth were we to meet such a major increase, and allow for a larger nursing establishment?

Staff changes compounded our problem. In July 1969 Dr Hartfield, who was Deputy Medical Superintendent, was asked by the Methodist Church to move to the Eastern Region and take charge of Ituk Mbang Methodist Hospital. Rehabilitation was desperately needed there in the wake of the Biafran civil war. In August, a few weeks delayed, I went on leave myself, and Dr Mulligan had to be Acting Medical Superintendent for the first time. It was not the easiest of times to take on such responsibility. After negotiations in September the government agreed to make up the proportion of the difference covered by their grant-in-aid, a maximum of 40% of the total. We had to find the rest from reserves. To my surprise the HMC in November accepted the budget for 1970 with a £24,700 deficit, but appointed a small committee to look at ways of increasing fees to meet it. We were on a slippery slope. Previously every single extra qualified nurse appointment had been looked at and costed with great care to be sure we could afford it. Now we had increased nursing staff by a total of 30, and faced a major upgrading of nurses' salaries into the bargain.

The unkindest cut was to come on the day in January when I returned from leave. The accountant, Jonathan Pope had decided to go. The MMS had found a place for him to serve in Cote-d'Ivoire and he was leaving the following day! He must have realised all too well the predicament the hospital was in. There was nothing for it but to take over the accounts myself, with the help of the Accounting Assistant, Mr M A Abiodun, and Mr Awodiya, and manage as best we could. It was only then that I realised the seriousness of our position. Jonathan had done well in improving the methods of accounting during his five years in charge, but as a result the accounts were a little more sophisticated compared with when the doctors and non-qualified staff had done them before. Having mastered the new methods there came the even more urgent need to revise the budget to reduce the deficit. £7000 was cut from expenditure on staff. Some measures to raise extra revenue were found, and the deficit reduced to £8,100; but that was not the end of it. Other problems were looming - and it was nine months before another accountant was found!

The free treatment scheme starts to near bankrupt the hospital
The new grant-aiding system was a block grant giving each hospital a proportion of their agreed annual estimates, the percentage depending on the size of the hospital (number of beds) the type of training (general nursing, midwifery or both) and the 'paediatric proportion'. We had moved away from a simple per-capita grant which the government would no longer accept. The new grant-aid system tried to simplify the payment for children under 18 by awarding so many points according to the proportion of children treated in relation to total numbers. If children's attendances were under 20% of all attendances, two points; 20–40% four points, and over 40% six points. With maximum points the grant ceiling was 40% of estimates. Smaller non-training centres scored fewer points and they were given a lower percentage.

The system was good, but with one draw-back. Ilesha's reputation for child health meant that we attracted young patients from far beyond the district catchment area. Eighty-five per cent of our out-patient attendances were under-eighteen and fifty-four per cent of our in-patients. All these visits, with consultation, investigations, medicines, and surgical procedures were free. The only thing paid for was the food each day if children were admitted into hospital. We were happy for our child patients, but there was a limit to the amount of cost-recovery we could get from the fifteen per cent adult out-patients and the forty-six per cent in-patients who were effectively subsidising the children. We tried to have the age limit changed to fourteen. The government refused. We tried to limit what was allowed free, and make a charge for such things as X-rays, certain operations and growth-charts. The government refused. We tried more than once to convince the government to increase the grant from 40% to 42%, a possibility included in the Ogunlesi Report. The government's Medical Advisory Committee agreed but the Executive refused. We tried reducing staff, but found that if we went below the required ratio of nurses to patients required for training, the tutors said the Nursing Council would stop us training. We were in a cleft stick. Initially the books were balanced by making every possible economy we could, and drawing on reserves. We had nothing then to meet contingencies. The Dutch Government increased our capital grant to meet some unavoidable overspending. The MMS paid £14,000 for the essential equipment for the new Maternity Department and £1500 for a staff house, and relieved us of those debts. The Methodist Church Nigeria promised N20,000 (£10,000) in 1973, but only managed the first instalment of N6000. We really were faced with the question as to whether a voluntary-agency hospital the size of Ilesha with a major nurse training programme, was sustainable. The MMS paid only for six missionary staff, accounting for under ten per cent of costs. All the rest had to come from local sources, government grants or adult patient fees.

Another cause for anxiety. Our surgeon retires

In June 1972 Dr Osmund Mulligan decided with great reluctance that he must go home for family reasons. His eldest son left at school in Ireland was desperately unhappy. Osmund was committed to life service, or for as long as the Methodist Church needed him, but in this matter he felt he had no choice, and all agreed with him. For the hospital it was a serious loss. He and his family had been with us since November 1964, eight years. He had learned Yoruba better than any of the expatriates, could preach in the language, and regularly took services in the chapel of Ifewara village. His surgery was widely respected, and enabled the hospital to be recognized for surgical training of registrars by Ibadan, London and Oxford. He had become well-known for his femoral or tibial osteotomy operations on children with deformities such as bow-legs and knock-knees, and in fact twenty per cent of all operations in 1970 were on children, (and therefore free!) From analysing his diagnostic punch-cards on in-patients (excluding under fives) he found that:

- hernia repair was the commonest operation, about 250 per year, and hernia patients top of the admissions list..................... 10.4%;
- abortions (spontaneous or the aftermath of those illegally procured) came next.. 9.4%;
- dysentery, anaemia and Ijesha shakes, each just above ....4%.

As in many hospitals depending largely on cost-recovery through fees, hernia operations were a major source of income, so we had that to thank Osmund for at this critical time. One of our Sisters, Mrs Akpan, had once been a theatre staff-nurse for Dr Harry Haigh at the Methodist Hospital, Ituk Mbang in eastern Nigeria, and reported that on his operating day he would do up to thirty hernia repairs, starting at 6.00 am. We never tried to emulate that! Harry was reputed to run the hospital on the proceeds.

The setback of Osmund's departure was mitigated when a friend of his, also a surgeon from Northern Ireland, offered to come. Six weeks later, in July 1972, Dr Crawford Bell, and his family arrived. He took on the work with great skill and dedication, but, unwittingly, with one drawback. He believed it was best to ration the number of hernias he would do by putting patients on a waiting list. Then he would have more time and beds for specialist surgical cases, especially the children's osteotomies as pioneered by Dr Mulligan. We had previously allowed hernia patients to be admitted in the same or the following week. When they were told to come back many weeks later they simply went over to the government general hospital (which opened in 1968), and had the operation done by Dr Gawad, their competent Egyptian doctor. WGH Ilesha's revenue dropped even further.

The government has its own troubles, and help to mission hospitals is threatened

The Western State government was anxious too, with escalating political demands and not enough revenue. A promise had been made to provide a government general hospital in every Local Government district where civil servants could be treated free. In October 1973 all the mission hospital leaders were called to the Ministry to be informed they were planning to cease supporting voluntary agency training programmes, and discontinue the Ogunlesi block grant system. Minor grants only

Fig 8.3 *The surgeon, Dr Osmund Mulligan, with his family*

would be paid. Strong pressure from all the mission hospitals, which together provided 38% of health services in the State for only one-tenth of the State health budget, was brought to bear. A very well reasoned petition was sent to the Military Governor in December 1973 refuting what the Ministry called 'a staggering increase' in the Block Grant. These had gone up from N426,000 in 1968–69 to N464,000 in 1972–73, despite inflation. In the same period the government estimates had gone up from N3.2 million to N9.4 million. Good sense prevailed. Normal grants were continued pro-tem, but the dangers remained.

Inflation was eating into people's ability to meet costs of ill health. Our fees had gone up as much as we felt fair, but numbers attending had dropped. The hospital with 193 beds showed a bed-occupancy rate of only 121. Reserves of N70,000 (£35,000) in 1971, dropped to N37,000 in 1972, N7000 in 1973, and were to go into the red by N50,000 in 1974. Dr Arun Baksi helped to organize a local 'Friends of Ilesha', with some influential Nigerians behind it who might hopefully produce some cash, but nothing substantial resulted. Mr David Scott, engineer husband of

Louise Scott, a missionary nurse appointed to Ikole, was co-opted as a management consultant to help examine all possibilities. We prayed earnestly to know what was the right thing to do.

Increasing insecurity and unrest

Few people appreciated what a precarious situation the hospital was in. In March 1974 the nurses threatened action unless they could be relieved of all non-nursing duties, presumably hoping the hospital would take on more maids for house-keeping functions. An Emergency HMC was called and calmed the air. The nurses agreed to cooperate.

It was not just in the hospital. There was unrest throughout the country that year. People's expectations were great. The oil boom was on, but the increasing inflation was biting into people's buying power. In the usual way, the Federal Government held the situation in check by appointing a Commission to investigate. Chaired by Mr Udoji, a senior civil servant, it sat for nearly twelve months. In January 1975 he presented his report. It recommended what seemed like a spectacular 100% rise in most salaries across the board, and what is more, decreed that the rise should be back-dated for a year! As a means of settling the unrest it secured a short-term respite. Those on salary scales determined by the government were highly pleased. Those running institutions were totally dismayed. The market-women selling yams and flour and salt simply doubled their prices to match, and the shops soon followed suit. Inflation soared. For us at WGH Ilesha the writing was on the wall. There was no way we could meet these new salary levels. A new destiny for the hospital had to be found, and found quickly.

CHAPTER 9

CRISIS, 1975

Considering the options

The hospital belonged to the Methodist Church Nigeria (MCN) so any decisions as to the future had to be made within the country, firstly by the Hospital Management Committee, and then finally by the church leadership. The hospital had for long followed a policy of working in close collaboration with the government at central and local level, and with the universities too, but without compromising its Christian emphasis. The Hospital Constitution defined the hospital's purpose very clearly:

> 'The purpose for which this hospital exists is, as a means of making known the love of God in Jesus Christ, to treat and care for the sick without discrimination as to race, tribe or religion, to promote a knowledge of health with a view to the prevention of disease, and to provide a training school for nurses, midwives and other personnel'.

As the love of God in Christ Jesus was for the poor, we did not feel it was open to us to simply go private, and charge fees so high that the poor would be denied all access. Cooperation with government, and the receipt of grants, had enabled us to at least treat all children without fees. Disease prevention through our mother and child care programme, and through immunisation campaigns as opportunity offered, had often seen the hospital pioneer new ways. Training was confirmed as a major function of the hospital through its expansion to meet nurse training requirements. The Dutch government grant had been secured on that premise, and we had an obligation to see that training remained central. We could not opt out and provide service only. So, which way to go?

Three possibilities presented themselves, affiliating in some way with University College Hospital, Ibadan, with which we had long had links; reaching an accommodation with the University of Ife and its new medical school which was just coming on stream; or integration into the government services as a general hospital of the Western State.

Ibadan university

Medical student postings from Ibadan University to Ilesha had been going since 1960. Relationships were close. Preliminary discussions with the Vice-Chancellor and Dean of the Medical Faculty about an even closer association did take place in November 1973. Professor T F Solanke, Ibadan's representative on the hospital's HMC, and Prof Jibril Aminu (Sub-Dean Clinical) were asked by Professor B O Osuntokun, then Dean, to visit Ilesha in August 1974, and prepare proposals. When these were tabled their concern was mainly how to increase the number of students assigned to Ilesha for clinical training, and the secondment of doctors to supervise. The first suggestion was ninety students, but we bargained it down to thirty-eight! A hostel big enough to hold them would be built. All medical schools were being pressed by the government at that time to increase their intake of students to the ridiculous figure of 1000 per year. The Deans tentatively accepted a figure of 500, but knew that even that was way beyond their capacity. The HMC in December looked at the Ibadan proposals, but saw there was nothing in them to undergird the hospital. A more radical scheme of action was needed if WGH was to survive. Professor Osuntokun agreed there was a case for 'WGH to be developed as an affiliated teaching hospital' but went on to explain 'This would take time to become effective....Under the present prevailing circumstances there is no means by which we can financially pay you a substantial subvention ...Tarry a little'.

But tarrying was no longer on the agenda.

Ife University

The background, and early contacts

Plans for the Western State to have a university to serve its own people were apparently first mooted at Independence in 1960. Although the University of Ibadan was in the State it had to serve the whole country. The first WGH links with the University of Ife (Unife, for short) began in 1966, when there was only an Ibadan Branch, with a School of Pharmacy and other Faculties on a campus adjacent to University of Ibadan (U.I.) A doctor from Ilesha was appointed to help plan the

University Health Centre to be built in Ife, and asked to say what consultant facilities WGH could provide when the move was made. The civil war (1967–1970) intervened, but after it was over building of the main campus at Ife, on a magnificent site with twenty-five square miles of land only twenty miles away from Ilesha, went ahead rapidly. There were plans for a Faculty of Health Sciences, with a medical school, and even in 1970 there was talk that WGH might become part of its 'teaching hospital complex'. This was reported by me in a Guild Hospital News letter in December 1970 with the comment, 'The opportunities are immense, and the responsibilities heavy'.

WGH brought into the picture

In January 1971 WGH was visited by an International Advisory Team of three professors from UK, Prof J L Stafford of London, Prof J M Bishop of Birmingham and Dr P H Fenton of Nottingham, together with Professor Ade Grillo (Department of Anatomy, University of Ibadan, but designated for Unife) and Mr I A Adebanjo, Senior Assistant Registrar for Unife. They were shown all the facilities at WGH Ilesha and were agreeably impressed. In June that year Professor Grillo was made the first Dean of the Faculty of Health Sciences.

Then WGH appointed its own sub-committee on Ife which met with Mr Adebanjo through 1971 and confirmed the hospital's willingness to cooperate. When a Faculty Board was formed in the following year, Dr Pearson was nominated to serve on it, the first meeting being in May 1972. It was at this meeting that Professor Grillo outlined the 'health team philosophy' which he intended to implement in the new Faculty. All members of the health team would be trained together for the early years and that would include doctors (40% of the students), dentists, nurses, and those studying the medical sciences, health engineering, nutrition and rehabilitation. They would then sit a BSc in basic health sciences and human biology, and only after that would they divide into their particular streams. He concluded:

> 'The cliché that the doctor is leader of the team must be suppressed. The doctor is no more unique than the centre-forward of a football team'.

By the initial training together he planned to promote this sense of equality. For the doctors there was to be a strong orientation towards Community Health, hopefully with half the curriculum devoted to it.

Though many of the ideas were modified as time went on, there was much in it to applaud, but also some cause for anxiety. As a professor of anatomy, and not a clinical doctor, it seemed that Professor Grillo was determined to cut the clinicians down to size. To say the least this did not promote good relationships with hospital colleagues.

The graduate nurse training issue

Having seen WGH Ilesha upgraded at such effort and expense to be eligible to train nurses to the equivalent of State Registered Nurse (SRN), and international recognition, it seemed folly to introduce a new style of graduate nurse-training on the American style so soon. In the University of Ibadan, there was already a post-basic BSc course which SRN nurses could sit in order to prepare themselves for higher posts as Nurse Tutors or Nursing Administrators. Ife was now proposing to have a basic nursing degree (BNSc) without having to be a diplomate nurse first. There was even talk of phasing out the diplomate training and having only graduate training for the Western State.

In the meantime the WGH HMC asked me to write to Professor Grillo in March 1972 to offer any help we could with the clinical teaching programme of the Ife medical students. When Professor Harold Rodgers arrived from Belfast to take up the chair of Surgery at Ife, and Professor Harrison from Liverpool for the chair in Pathology later that year, an active programme of joint clinical meetings began.

Anxiety over the nursing issue did not go away, and proved to be widespread. In April 1972 six of the senior medical consultants in Adeoyo State Hospital in Ibadan wrote to the Ministry of Health to 'raise the alarm' about the proposed new philosophy at Ife.

> 'The basic philosophy should be changed; nurses and paramedical staff should be given diplomate, and <u>not</u> graduate training.'

The letter was tabled at the Faculty Board, but I was dismayed to see it brushed aside. My own comment, which I put in the margin of the Minutes, concerned 'the overwhelming need of the country is for diplomate nurses, not graduates. The country may need cars, but very few people can afford a Mercedes-Benz. First produce enough Morris Minors for all.'

Fig 9.1 *International advisory team from Ife come on a visit to Ilesha, January 1971. Left to right: Prof Bishop, Prof Stafford, Dr Akinkugbe, Mr Adebanjo, Dr Fenton and Prof Grillo*

Fig 9.2 *The medical staff in 1974. Left to right: Dr Stephen Mathai, Dr Christine Baski, Dr Crawford Bell, Dr Jenny Mee, Dr Arun Baski, Dr 'Bode Akintade, Dr Andrew Pearson and Dr Mary Thwaites*

An Advisory Panel on the BNSc programme was set up by the University Senate, and many people sent in their comments, for or against. Mr Babajide, our Principal Tutor at Ilesha was in favour, so long as the BNSc was side by side with the diplomate programme. Professor Fabian Udekwu, Chairman of the National Voluntary Agencies Medical Advisory Committee, was mainly against, and my own comments, and those of Dr Brian McGucken, my then Deputy Med Supt, were for the graduate programme to be Post-Basic. In October 1972 I corresponded with Dr S L Adesuyi, Chief Medical Adviser to the Federal government, asking his advice, and he replied,

> 'With regard to the matter of training of graduate nurses, I share the same views as you have expressed. For the same reason, we in this Ministry have discouraged the establishment of graduate training in Basic Nursing in Ibadan University. We are able to do this because Ibadan University is a Federal Institution. Ife University however is a State Institution over which we have no control. However the matter is still being discussed and I do hope that it is not too late to effect a change.'

At the next meeting of the Ife Faculty Board on 12th Jan 1973 I expressed myself strongly in favour of the diplomate programme as the most suitable one for the Western State, and urged Ife to make the graduate programme a Post-Basic degree as in Ibadan. Though it was agreed that the diplomate programme should continue in the State, a Post-Basic degree was felt by the Dean to be against the entire ethos of the Faculty with its health team approach. I had touched a very tender nerve. The debate continued, but did not change the situation further, except that Professor Grillo apparently took my opposition very personally, so that relationships became strained. Perhaps I made a mistake in being so outspoken, and insisting afterwards that my dissent should be recorded, but that was how I, and many others, felt.

I also wrote to the Vice-Chancellor of Unife, Professor Oluwasanmi, an agriculturist, and urged that the matter be referred to the Nursing Council of Nigeria and the National Council on Health, concluding by saying:

> 'Forgive me if I appear critical on this particular point. In general I believe the Faculty is going ahead in an exciting way, and recruiting

> an excellent teaching staff, and I am glad to be associated with it, even if on the sidelines'.

He replied reassuringly on 5th May, saying:

> 'I fully understand, and indeed, share much of your concern about the Basic Nursing degree course which we are planning to establish, and I am very appreciative of the consideration which made you write to me. ....This is an experiment which we feel is overdue, and which, having considered the pros and cons, including most of those you have raised, we have undertaken to try'.

The debate was at a gentlemanly and rational level.

Cooperation grows, but uncertainty remains

Through the rest of 1973 and in 1974 cooperation did grow in many ways, particularly through Dr Isaac Abayomi of Unife's Division of Community Care and plans to follow up the Imesi-Ile research. Dr Abayomi also helped at WGH and looked after the TB Clinic for a period while I was on leave.

Professor M A Bankole, who was made Sub-Dean for MB.ChB Studies in January 1974, clarified the situation a little by explaining that, as a university under State auspices, they were planning to send their medical and nursing students to the State hospitals for clinical experience, but did not have any control over the hospitals, or input into them. 'The University will not receive any direct funds for clinical facilities....In the circumstances, any ties we have with WGH would be professional and educational only, not administrative or financial'.

Certainly Ife had problems, but in view of the growing financial predicament at WGH this did not seem very promising. Professor Grillo was away from Ife for quite a long time and no letter had been received from him since June 1972.

In May 1974 a more formal memorandum from the WGH HMC was sent to the Vice-Chancellor of Unife pointing out the many strong points which the hospital could offer as a base for teaching, and hoping that a link with financial implications could be forged. It was noted that the medical school of the university in Zaria was making an educational subvention to the Anglican Hospital at Wusasa for the use of its facilities. I wrote:

> 'WGH is not ashamed to be known as a Christian hospital, though we would be the first to admit our many failings. The atmosphere is tolerant and non-sectarian.... I do not think it would be out of place for a University Faculty to enter into some kind of joint administration with such a hospital. Surely the big unsolved problem of medical educationists is how to instil a *motivation for service* in the doctors they produce. Such a motivation is more easily caught than taught, and if the environment of Wesley Guild Hospital can contribute a little in this process one of our main purposes will have been fulfilled.
>
> If this is to happen, then action needs to be taken now... The hospital has undertaken to find a solution by July 1974. If none is forthcoming the whole structure of the Hospital may have to be reduced, phasing out midwifery and nursing training, and continuing, if we can, as a minor service institution. No one on the staff believes that course is right. All are keen to continue the training emphasis. Only the sheer facts of finance would force the other on us, and some would rather we close than see that day. Our future is in the balance. Is Unife interested?'.

The Vice-Chancellor assured us that a definite decision had been taken to include WGH in the teaching hospital complex. The date for a final decision by HMC on the hospital's future was deferred to December 1974. Contact was at last resumed with Professor Grillo and attempts made, without great success, to mend relationships. I reported to him that the HMC had resolved to invite Unife to appoint a representative, and Professor Grillo was himself nominated to come.

The point of decision - Ibadan, or Ife?

On 7th December 1974 a Special HMC was called to decide finally whether WGH should affiliate with Ife or with Ibadan. Professor Grillo was away on WHO business, and Professor Bankole came in his place. Professor Solanke put the proposals from the University of Ibadan, but recognized that Ife had the geographical advantage. Ibadan would build and finance a student hostel, and provide educational equipment, but could offer no grant to keep the hospital running, effectively therefore ruling itself out. Professor Bankole for Ife said that they envisaged two kinds of hospital in relation to their proposed teaching hospital complex; Category A, fully and totally under the Board, and Category B, those affiliated with loose representations bilaterally. He thought WGH would wish to remain in Category B, and might hope to attract national funds for teaching hospitals from the Federal Government. If WGH opted for Category A it would be run and financed by Unife's Board. WGH staff felt that the financial implications were still vague, but agreed to produce a projection of likely costs for the next HMC.

Integration into government services

This third possibility had been around since 1966 when 'Combined Hospital' status for hospitals in receipt of grants had been proposed, but now, as we entered 1975, it became a very immediate issue. It was to be a traumatic year. The government had successfully applied a wage freeze for three years, except for the Elwood increase for nurses. In early January the Western State government announced it was accepting the Udoji recommendations of the Federal Government for a 100% increase in salaries, backdated to April 1974. Expectations were naturally great. The voluntary hospitals throughout Nigeria had to appeal to their respective State governments for help. Health matters were all dealt with at that level. The States in turn had to wait for guidance and financial help from the Federal government.

The Western State call for hand-over in return for funding

On February 25th 1975 the Ministry of Health, Ibadan called representatives of all the church-related hospitals in the Western State together to announce their decision to give full funding to all on condition the churches agreed to hand over proprietorship to a State Health Council, into which all government hospitals would also be entering. The State would be divided into eight Zones, with a Hospital Management Board for each. The Zone for Ilesha would have a special relationship with the University of Ife, and be part of its teaching hospital complex. The Ministry stressed their wish that the hospitals keep their names and Christian character 'to ensure continuance of their customary efficiency and esprit de corps'. So, take-over in all but name, it was to be. No details were put in writing, but an answer accepting in principle was requested within three weeks. None of the hospitals really had much choice, and the various proprietors, Catholic, Baptist, Anglican, Seventh Day Adventist and Methodist submitted letters of acceptance, expecting for the sake of their staff and the patients who depended on them that money would come soon.

Negotiations with the government as to what we would consider as our 'Religious rights' took place. For Wesley Guild Hospital these were formulated to include:

* retention of the hospital's name and purpose, as in the Constitution.

* allowing the Hospital Chapel to continue, the Hospital Chaplain to remain in the house adjacent to the chapel; time for staff prayers in the chapel, and worship for patients in wards and elsewhere.

* the Methodist Church Nigeria be allowed to nominate for the posts of Medical Superintendent, Matron and Hospital Secretary, and any other posts for whom suitable missionary-minded personnel might be found.

* the general life of the community living on the compound should conform to Christian standards.

Crisis time

Lightning strike

There had been other developments meantime. Professor Grillo was back from his travels, and the politics was turning nasty. He was not pleased with Dr Pearson for speaking out against his plans for graduate nurse training, and he was going to take action. The kid gloves were off, and there was undoubtedly manipulation of the nursing school leaders behind the scenes.

We have to go back to January. On Saturday, January 25th the HMC met with the President of the Methodist Church, the Rev. Professor Bolaji Idowu, in the chair for the first time. He was rightly there because of the critical importance of the occasion. The future of the hospital was at stake. Professor Grillo also attended for the first time. He used the opportunity to criticize Dr Pearson for what he felt had been 'discourteous' behaviour, presumably for opposing the BNSc programme in his Faculty Board, and going over his head to the Vice-Chancellor, though this was not explained. He put the case for merger with Ife. Staff members on the Committee also pressed hard for some definite commitment to be made towards Ife as a means of solving the economic problems, but the President refused to be stampeded and appointed a small committee to consider the matter - a normal Methodist solution. The situation was not, however, normal. The President had not realised the tinder dry position we were in. A long and tiring meeting lasting from 10.00 am to 7.00 pm closed in uncertainty and doubt, *with no decision.* This was the fateful spark. At 8.00 pm that night the Nigeria Nurses Association, led by Mr Babajide the Principal Tutor, and Mrs Titi Ajanaku, Midwifery Tutor, took the entire nursing body (including students) off the wards, leaving women in labour, children on drips, and over 150 patients totally uncared for. The effect was devastating, and many senior staff were deeply disturbed. Dr Crawford Bell handed in his resignation as Deputy Medical Superintendent to the President that night while he was resting in my house. In remonstrating verbally with him, he put a hand to his shoulder, and the President interpreted that as a physical attack. He was afraid for his personal safety and would not stay at the hospital, but asked to be taken to the Superintendent minister's house in the town. According to Mr M.M. Familusi's history of the Methodist Church Nigeria, there were rumours on the church compound that hospital staff would be assassinated. This was, of course, without foundation, but shows how charged the situation was.

Picking up the pieces

For the next four days and nights the missionary sisters, doctors, the two Nigerian housemen, Dr Dominic and Dr Ebiekpi, medical students and Joan Wright, a retired teacher visiting us from Britain, all worked a roster to man the wards 24 hours in the day. Teams were formed with one doctor, one nurse, and one other for each shift. Mrs Pearson looked after the tea and coffee, and kept all the teams supplied with refreshment - until she was laid low with a slipped disc, and was out of action for a month. Reports were brought to us that the nurses had been parading around the town carrying a makeshift coffin labelled, 'Dr Pearson, R.I.P. On January 29th the small committee met, but with a leading Methodist layman, Mr J.O. Ogunseitan, taking the place of the Chairman, the Rev. Fowode, who was unavoidably absent in Benin. The

President did not come again. The meeting constituted itself as an Emergency HMC. Professor Grillo was there, and observers from the unions and Mr E.A. Ifaturoti representing Friends of WGH. After looking at all the possibilities, and realising a decision would have to be approved by Methodist Conference, it was finally agreed that a letter be written saying that WGH wished to become one of the teaching hospitals of the Unife Hospital Board, with the rider that it was hoped that the Hospital could retain its name, and its character as a Christian institution. With that letter in hand Professor Grillo said he would persuade the Ministry to release money for the payment of the new Udoji salaries. The union representatives were content and the strike was called off.

Missionary reaction

The staff returned. Work was resumed, and a week later Dr Howard Souster of the MMS fortuitously arrived for a visit planned well before. He found many of the missionary staff still hurt and angry that the Nurses Association, led by nurse tutors, could shelter behind the protection of 'Union rights of protest' despite the damage they had done to the hospital, and to the reputation of their profession by the total and precipitate abandonment of their patients. Those who were thinking of staying on longer decided not to. Dr Bell, Dr and Mrs (Dr) Baksi and Dr Thwaites had gone by April, and Mr Beyer's tour ended a few weeks later. Dr Mee and Dr Stephen Mathai were to go in June or July. Dr Dominic and Dr Ebiekpi, fearing reprisals for having worked through the strike, went at once. Only Doreen Habbershaw, Matron, and myself, unable to contemplate the imminent collapse of WGH after having been there so long, kept our minds open, praying for some clear indication as to whether to go or stay. What was quite evident to us both was that, in the present political climate, a Nigerian medical superintendent should take charge within a year.

The second strike

The situation continued to be fraught. March came and ended - no money. April came - still nothing. Notice was given to staff that the hospital might have to close on May 31st if no grant arrived. On April 18th we learned that the Methodist President's letter to the Ministry in Ibadan concerning WGH's entry to the State Health Council and special relationship with Unife, had not been considered a sufficiently definite acceptance. 'It was too much like a sermon', one official said. Negotiations to persuade the President to write another letter were protracted.

The Owa of Ijeshaland, not himself a Christian, sent a powerful delegation to the President threatening a curse on his home. The nurses' union representatives tried their persuasion, but without success, so on May 9th they called a 'work to rule' to start the following day. Matron and I interpreted this as another strike in all but name.

Having this time given notice as required by Nigerian trade union law, even though it was only one day, we felt we could not risk a re-run of January, and asked the doctors to discharge or transfer all the in-patients. On May 10th the striking nurses found the hospital empty. I guess their leaders were angry and confused as to what to do next, and many of the nurses were surging around the administration block, as I was about to enter my office that morning. Just then a highly respected visitor from the town, Mrs J.E. Fajemisin, a keen member of Friends of WGH, turned up in her car to ask me a question. The answer required a return home, so I turned round and we went back together through the crowd, now very restless. It was reported that the hospital's main front gate, and the side gate, were locked and guarded, and that the other senior staff were being confined to the Administration Block and not allowed to leave. It seemed my unexpected visitor had thwarted the leader's plan. The Medical Superintendent was the only hospital officer not in his office! Then came the moment when Mr Sam Akpaete, a senior laboratory worker, ran to warn us that the nurses, now quite out of hand, were 'coming to get Dr Pearson'. My wife and I decided it was best for us to be out of the way to defuse tension, and withdrew quickly over the barbed-wire back fence of the hospital compound, Jean tearing her leg in the process. We walked - or limped - to the house of Mrs Komolafe, Deputy Matron, which was close by in the town to wait with Zacchaeus, her husband, till things simmered down. A friend took us to Pastor Sydney Elton's house for the night. Our whereabouts was not known to the strikers, but we could communicate with Dr Baksi in the hospital through the private phone line which he had just had installed. The following day we went to Ibadan and joined in the final negotiations between Church and State. Justice Olu Ayoola, of Ilesha (and also the MCN Vice-President), found a formula for the additional letter agreeable to the President, and this was accepted by the Commissioner for Health, who also agreed to talk severely to the strike leaders. They were summoned to the Ministry of Health in Ibadan next day, warned against 'lawlessness', and a cheque for 'Udoji arrears' issued. Salaries for April, May and June, were accepted as a debt upon the government, not upon the Mission. The strike was over - but a die had been cast.

The end of direct missionary participation

Returning to Ilesha next day the process of re-opening the hospital began, a slow business cleaning up the mess, and an even slower task to regain the confidence of patients. Doreen and I were now quite sure the time had come to leave. She put in her resignation, the end of 13 years sterling service (1962–1975). I submitted mine too, quite ready for a change after 23 years (1952–1975). An invitation to work with the University of Ibadan had been delivered to me by Professor Betty Topley of Igbo-Ora on the very evening of the second strike, while we were at the Elton's house in town. Professor Osuntokun, the Dean, asked that, should I ever think of leaving Ilesha, would I consider coming to Igbo-Ora, Ibadan's rural branch campus, 'to help direct the students towards a generalist vocation'. I felt God was in the calling, and sent a provisional acceptance. As one door was closing, another was opening. Negotiations with Dr Sam Olowe, one of our first pre-registration doctors, now a consultant paediatrician in Lagos, and a Methodist, were put in hand to see if he would come in my place as Medical Superintendent.

Looking back one felt that the break need not have been so traumatic and devastating. Initial approaches from both sides, covering nearly ten years, had been so promising. Clinical cooperation between WGH and Ife had been growing steadily. If only the negotiations had remained on a 'gentlemanly and rational' basis how much richer could have been the association. But there it was. Radical change is rarely smooth. We could but affirm our faith that 'all things work together for good, to them that love God'.

Informing the home church

Every effort was made to explain the situation clearly, both to the Methodist Church in Nigeria, and to the MMS in Britain. I was concerned that the Methodist newspaper in U.K., the *Methodist Recorder* should carry the news, and Pauline Webb, the Africa Secretary, had prepared an article. However, out of sensitivity for relationships with the Rev. Bolaji Idowu, President of the church in Nigeria, the Rev. Colin Morris, the MMS General Secretary at the time, in full consultation with the headquarters team, suggested it be withheld. He hoped the President himself would write, but he never brought himself to do so. After the eighty-three years of support from the Wesley Guild and Methodists in Britain, I felt they deserved better. Relationships between the Rev. Bolaji Idowu and the church in Britain remained strained for many

Fig 9.3 *Dr Pearson planting a coconut before departure in 1975. Mrs Pearson, the chaplain Revd Oguntuase, Matron Mrs Komolafe and other staff members look on*

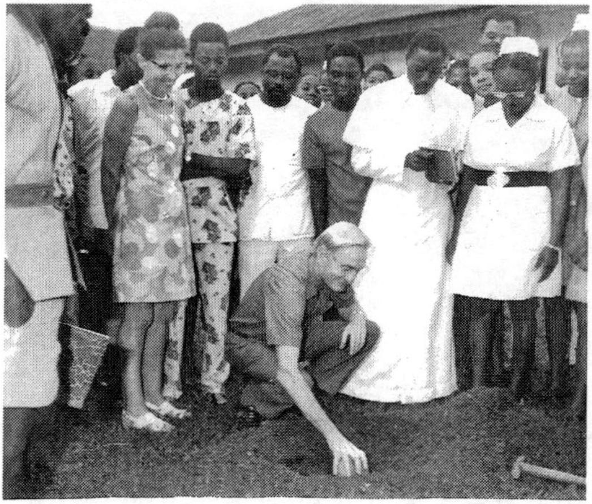

years, and the policy of 'least said, soonest mended' became the rule. Fortunately all is well today with a new Methodist leader in place in Nigeria, His Eminence the Rev. Sunday Mbang.

Interim arrangements, and farewells

After the departure of missionary staff from WGH in April invaluable help came from the Departments of Obstetrics and Surgery in Ibadan with the secondment of specialist staff. So many had a deep appreciation of the hospital, and did not want to see it die. Ife too began to second medical staff, and there was a hope that two more doctors from India whom I had recruited would arrive before too long. Negotiations with Dr Sam Olowe were continuing.

An invitation to my wife and me for a Farewell party on June 25th came from the leaders of the Nigeria Nurses Association, an indication of where power in the hospital now effectively lay. The tail seemed to be wagging the dog! As this appeared to be the official farewell, I gently refused to accept the invitation unless it came from the hospital management. The letter was hurriedly changed and brought back over the name of Mr Awodiya. No one really felt like partying, so it was not the easiest of occasions. Gifts and speeches were exchanged. Efforts were made to mend fences. The next day Mr Awodiya invited me to plant a coconut in the ground between the Chapel and the Admission Room, saying,

> 'This will grow into a palm-tree, symbol of long life, prosperity and peace, and be a reminder of Dr Pearson's time in Ilesha.'

On our last week-end the Methodist Church called my wife and me and Doreen to a Valedictory Service in Otapete Church to express thanks and present gifts. The church's Farewell Address ended on a note of faith.

> 'It is our hope that, as the reward of good work is more work, you would go into a new sphere of medical service where your energy and abilities will have fuller scope, even while we are sorry to lose you from amongst us.....Wherever you go, take with you our good-will and our friendship, and may God watch you and protect you and all yours in His mighty arms of love.'

It remained just to complete the 1974/75 Hospital Report. All the material was gathered up and compiled before I left, but its printing in Ibadan, and distribution from Ilesha had to be done by others towards the end of the year. My last Medical Superintendent's resumé of the year was difficult to write, but concluded hopefully:

> 'The new chapter in the hospital's history under the State Health Council, Western State, Nigeria has begun. Though under Nigerian leadership there will still be room for the international element in medical staffing, and people of many countries will be watching developments. We pray that the world-wide reputation of the Hospital will be enhanced, and a genuine Christian spirit will inspire all who serve in Ilesha in the years to come.'

CHAPTER 10

UNDER NEW MANAGEMENT, 1975–1995

Within the State Health Council

Mr Awodiya in charge pro-tem

From July 1st 1975, when my wife and I departed from Ilesha with the last of our loads, the hospital was effectively under new management. Doreen Habbershaw handed over the nursing administration to Mrs Rebecca Komolafe as the new Matron, and to Mrs Dorothy Ogedengbe as Deputy Matron, and left a few days later after fulfilling a promise to be present at the 1975 gathering of the Nurses' League. Unfortunately I had no senior doctor left at WGH to hand over to, and Mr Awodiya the Manager, together with Mr Niyi Adeyemi, who had been my very efficient Confidential Secretary, and Mr M A Abiodun, Accountant, carried on the general administration as best they could.

A personal viewpoint from the side-lines

The story from this point on is largely second-hand through letters and reports, but also from occasional visits. After three months leave in Britain, Jean and I returned to Nigeria, but this time I was employed by the College of Medicine, Ibadan, working as Chief Medical Officer for the Community Health programme, and resident at the branch campus at Igbo-Ora, 75 miles west of Ibadan. We were still within 150 miles of Ilesha, and our first visit back was in November 1975.

Nigeria had been through another military coup, and General Gowon was replaced by Muritala Mohammed on July 29th, and all commissioners at Federal and State level had been relieved of their posts. It was an uneasy time, and this was reflected in the hospital. Decisions were not being made. Dr Sam Olowe had agreed in principle to come from Lagos to be Medical Superintendent, but the new State Health Council, and the Ministry of Health, had still been unable to agree on the terms of employment. As a possible alternative, the final HMC on June 21st sent an invitation to Dr S O Franklin, a senior physician and a Methodist who had just retired from the Ministry of Health, Ibadan. He was not able to accept, so hopes still lay with Dr Olowe. A UK visitor, Dr David Cundall, grandson of the missionary, Dr Edward Cundall, with whom I had worked in China, came in July for two months, and overlapped with Dr Jenny Mee and Mr Steve Athey, pharmacist, the last two of the missionary team who left at the end of July. He was impressed with the possibilities at WGH, despite all the knocks, and felt, very irreverently, that the teaching of Ife medical school would come to no harm if it were ' transferred lock, stock and Grillo to Ilesha!'

More doctors arrive

Unife did try to fill the staffing gap, and seconded a medical couple, who were with them, to come to WGH for three days each week. Dr Bob Brown and Mrs Brown, one a surgeon and the other an anaesthetist (both supported by the aid group 'Hope Project') did much to keep the surgical services going. The Ministry sent Dr Craig, a Dutch trained Nigerian gynaecologist, and Dr Odetoyinbo, just registered; so, one way or another the hospital was kept going. There was much prayer by the staff, and they felt there had been a real answer when the two Indian doctors, Dr Alexander Pothan and Dr P K Alexander, arrived in September. Mr Niyi Adeyemi wrote to me about their arrival and said,

> They 'asked a funny question. Where is that Dr Pearson?'

So much had happened since I had sent them appointment papers. However, all credit to them; they stayed and provided excellent service, one for six months, and the other for two years.

'Integrated' administration

In August 1975 Mr Awodiya resisted a demand from the Ministry to remit all WGH revenue to the State Health Council as was the normal procedure for government general hospitals. With such uncertainties at top level he knew there was no way the government could cope with the different style of administration at Ilesha. His fight was successful. A type of 'integrated administration' was developed for WGH, and also for the other mission hospitals in the State Health Council. The State paid salaries, and the fee income was retained for running costs. The church remained the proprietor. Full takeover was never consummated in the

Western State. Other States varied in their response to the situation, some with fuller takeover, others with barely any interference or support at all.

Federal government take-over

Before the end of the year, there had been yet another military coup. Some sudden decisions were made. Ife University was taken by the Federal Government from the Western State, and an Ife University Teaching Hospital Complex (IUTHC) was promulgated by decree incorporating Ife State Hospital, Ife Seventh Day Adventist Hospital, Ilesha General Hospital, and Ilesha Wesley Guild Hospital. The two government and two mission hospitals were thus summarily expropriated, without negotiation, by the publishing of a military edict in the Federal Government Gazette. The State government was not pleased, but could do little about it. The church proprietors were simply resigned to whatever came. The high-handed action did however secure the release of funds from the Federal Government which was the accepted channel for university teaching hospitals, so the change was a blessing in disguise. A major draw-back was that WGH was not allowed to remain a member of the Christian Health Association of Nigeria, and thus to receive cheap drugs from CHANPHARM which would have been such a boon to patients.

Changes in the local church, but contacts with WGH maintained

In January 1976 the Methodist Church Nigeria adopted a new constitution with Bishops, four Archbishops and a Patriarch as the church's head, so different from the more modest pattern of the Methodist church in Britain. His Pre-eminence Professor Bolaji Idowu, the main architect of the scheme, was invested as the first Patriarch at a service at Tinibu Methodist Cathedral, Lagos, which lasted nine hours! The organist, Rob Harris, had to be plied with drinks and sandwiches to maintain his strength! Ilesha became the head of one Archdiocese stretching east to Owo and north to Kwara, and the Rev. E A Fowode was inducted as Archbishop. He was a great help to Mr Awodiya who felt he was running WGH almost single-handed.

A Methodist minister had been moved into the house close to the hospital chapel during 1975, and his presence as Chaplain to the hospital was accepted. The Chapel continued to be used for morning prayers, but the timing had to be before duty hours, not as the first fifteen minutes of the hospital day. Nurses' fellowship groups used the chapel for week-night meetings, and the Sunday services run by the Chaplain served people in the Ijofi area, whether members of hospital staff or not. The opportunity to use the minister's appointment as the equivalent of a university chaplaincy was perhaps not fully appreciated by the Methodist Church at that time. More could have been done. However real tribute is due to the nursing staff at all levels who kept the spirit of Christian dedication alive during those difficult days.

Ife administration starts to be felt

The University of Ife began advertising medical staff vacancies in February 1976 and among the first service doctors to arrive were Dr Bayo Ademowore who had specialised in obstetrics in the United States, and Dr F.F. Bishara, a physician from Egypt. None of the Ife university teaching consultants were prepared to move over to Ilesha. Dr Ademowure took on the role of Acting Medical Superintendent. In March 1976 Professor Michael Bankole was elected Dean of the Faculty of Health Sciences at Ife in place of Professor Ade Grillo who retired from the scene. Professor Harold Rogers wrote to say 'a cloud seems to have lifted'. There is no doubt Professor Grillo had a vision of a community-orientated style of training which was making headway in many other countries around the world. However, few of the Faculty staff that had been appointed really shared his vision, nor his style of putting his ideas over. A change of leadership was therefore welcomed.

Mr Awodiya reaches retirement age

The Board of the Teaching Hospital Complex was quasi-independent of the university, and had its own style of administration, with a non-medical Director of Administration as executive head. There were to be no more Medical Superintendents, and the senior doctor became just Chief Consultant in an advisory role. In July 1976 Mr Abiodun was informed that he should take temporary charge as Acting Unit Administrator until the substantive holder, Mr Ige, arrived, and Mr Awodiya was given only one month's notice of termination despite his thirty-six years service. Little did people realise what sterling work Hezekiah had done. I attended his farewell meeting at Ilesha in November where many words of appreciation were given for his long service. In a reply speech Mr Awodiya appealed to the Director of Administration to cooperate with all the (ex-mission) staff to achieve their desire which is their future security. Everyone was very concerned. Pension rights were not being recognized. To the staff themselves he urged that

> 'they should stay clear of bribery and corruption which was totally forbidden by the hospital authorities (in his time), and to avoid crisis (tactics) and demand their rights in a constitutional way'.

He had endured more than his fair share of union disputes. A brown envelope was then handed to him by the Unit Administrator in appreciation of his services. He opened it and showed the cheque to me on the side. It turned out to be an ex-gratia payment equivalent to a mere one month's salary. I almost cried.

The disappointment of the Ilesha community

After some years all Federal-funded teaching hospitals changed to having a Chief Medical Director (CMD) in overall charge, with Directors of Clinical Services, Nursing and Administration at the next level. Ife followed the same line, but without benefit to WGH. The CMD tended to concern himself primarily with Ife State Hospital. The people of Ilesha were disappointed that the link with a university brought so little benefit to the town. It seemed to them that the IUTHC was stripping Wesley Guild of its assets, including staff and laboratory equipment, and not putting much back. Mr Theophilus Olawoye, on whom such hopes had been placed to maintain the standards of the laboratory after his further training in England, could not take it, and left. All consultants lived twenty miles away at Ife, leaving only junior resident doctors at WGH. Clinical standards suffered. One obstetrician from Ife was appointed, and offered an Ilesha hospital house, the one which had been used by the Medical Superintendent. He accepted, but continued to live in Ife, using the Ilesha house instead as his private hospital. No-one could stop him because he was related to a prominent Ife chief. Morale fell to the lowest ebb. Mrs Komolafe, the Matron, used often to look back and recall the days when Wesley Guild Hospital was in its hey day as a church institution and (as she put it) 'When Wes-er-ley was Wes-er-ley'.

The nurses stand firm, and many of the old staff remain

Not all was lost. The nursing service in particular maintained good discipline, punctuality and high standards. The Principal Tutor and staff of the Nursing School were told in no uncertain terms by the leaders of the Nursing Council of Nigeria that the engineering of strikes, such as they had undertaken, was entirely unacceptable. The damage they had done had been incalculable. The authority of the Matron's office, and that of the Hospital as a whole, was to be accepted unconditionally. Relationships improved.

Most of the clerical and labour staff remained at their posts giving devoted service as they had always done. The electrician, mechanics and carpenters maintained the buildings and equipment in good working order. On the campus, the land between the wards was looked after, ice-plant hedges trimmed, grass kept mown, and everywhere tidy. Eman Fakuade took pride in seeing that garden maintenance continued precisely as he had been taught by Mrs Pearson. Between the houses, at the residential end of the compound, it was a different matter. The land there was considered to be the responsibility of the house-holders as in the older universities, whereas under the church it had been a matter of shared care. Labour staff were told not to go there any more. No grass was cut, no hedges trimmed or pruned, and the bush grew all around. It was some years later before the hospital administration realised they were rendering the houses barely habitable, and once again took the whole area in hand.

WGH as seen from Igbo-Ora

The full history of the twenty years since takeover up to the present day, 1975 to 1995, can only be told with accuracy by those at present in charge. For ten of those years I was to remain in the country and keep in touch, and Jean and I have made several visits since. There was always a warm welcome.

General practice training, based on WGH Ilesha experience
From 1975 to 1983 my work as Chief Medical Officer for the Ibarapa Community Health Programme involved service work as a district doctor in the 10-bed Health Centre in Igbo-Ora, and the 36-bed hospital at Eruwa, 20 miles away. It also involved teaching general practice to the medical students of College of Medicine, Ibadan who came for a six-weeks residential posting during their fourth year. The experience gained at WGH Ilesha proved an ideal basis for teaching the practical

clinical skills necessary in rural medicine. The students were enthusiastic learners. General Practice had never been taught as such before. They welcomed it and went further, saying that they also needed a postgraduate General Practice training programme for a Fellowship in that discipline. If it were organized on a similar basis to the Fellowship programmes in other specialities, such as Surgery or Ophthalmology or Pathology, many said that would be the career they would wish to choose.

The Dean of the Medical Faculty, Professor Osuntokun, encouraged the development of such a programme, and after much consultation with other academics and leaders of General Practice in the country, I produced a draft curriculum and a suggested course structure, with the support of the Association of General Medical Practitioners of Nigeria (AGMPN) In 1979, when a National Postgraduate Medical College was inaugurated, a provisional General Practice Faculty Board was formed from AGMPN members, including myself, and its first duty was to submit the curriculum to national debate. A Conference was called in Ibadan in March 1980, and the AGMPN-backed curriculum was looked at by workshops and in plenary session, and finally approved by general consensus with only minor modifications. It had been expected that the College of Medicine, Ibadan, would be the base from which training would take place, but the Deanship had changed. Professor Osuntokun had handed over to Professor Akande. Moreover, the national and university financial situation was less stable. A residency programme in General Practice was turned down in favour of Dentistry and Pharmacy for which external funding was immediately available. It looked as if the GP training programme would be still-born.

The possibility that WGH would be returned to the Methodist Church

It was at this time that the Ife Faculty of Health Sciences, under Professor Bankole's deanship, had decided that four hospitals were not necessary for inclusion in the Teaching Hospital Complex. Two would be sufficient, and the assumption was that the two to be retained would be the government institutions, Ife State Hospital, and Ilesha General Hospital. The possibility therefore arose that WGH Ilesha would be returned to the Methodist Church Nigeria. The State Health Council informed the church to be ready to receive the hospital. The Governor of the Western State, Mr Bola Ige (generally known as 'Uncle Bola') was briefed, but nothing put in writing. The senior Methodist minister in

Ilesha, now His Grace the Archbishop, the Most Rev. T A Akinigbagbe, approached me to see if I would be interested to come back to WGH for one year to put the hospital on to its feet as a church institution once again. I was called to discuss the matter with him in the presence of the Governor at the State Secretariat. Bola hinted there was nothing settled. I said that I would be prepared to consider WGH on one condition, namely that the hospital should opt to be a training hospital for General Practice residents. The matter was therefore put to the three senior Ife physicians currently mostly concerned with Ilesha. It happened they were all paediatricians, Dr Kayode Olamijulo, Dr Kabba Joiner and Dr Oyedeji, and they were unanimous that if WGH was released from its present purpose of training medical students to be doctors, they believed the hospital could take on the role of training young doctors to be first rate General Practitioners. Their proposal paper was placed before the Postgraduate College Faculty Board for General Medical Practice and unanimously accepted. The Board said gratefully that this was precisely the kind of hospital which they wanted to use for training, and added that if WGH Ilesha proved acceptable after inspection, then similar hospitals should also be invited to apply, such as Baptist Hospital Ognomosho, Iyi Enu Hospital Onitsha, and Mkar Hospital Gboko by way of example.

Ilesha hopes dashed, but postgraduate training for General Practice goes ahead

The change of Dean at Ibadan College of Medicine had provided us with one set-back. Now the Deanship at Ife changed - yet again! How much can depend on who is in charge! Professor Michael Bankole's four year term came to an end, and Professor Ade Grillo was re-elected for a second time. I guessed at once that WGH Ilesha would not be released, and that turned out to be the case. However, since the GP Faculty Board had considered the acceptability of WGH, and also other large mission hospitals, as centres for training, the way was still open for the other centres to apply. They did. They were inspected and accepted, and the GP residency programme was able to go ahead after all. The first GP Primary examinations were in 1981, the first Part I Finals in 1983, and the first Part II Finals in 1985. By that time there were forty-two Training Hospitals, Part I and II, and seventy registrars in training. The most active and successful training centres turned out to be the mission hospitals, and without them the GP residency programme would never have taken off so quickly. One of the first two doctors to pass and become a Fellow in General Practice of the National Postgraduate Medical College of Nigeria (FMCGP) was Dr E A (Tunde) Kuteyi, and he joined the Ife university teaching hospital complex as Consultant in General Practice, taking responsibility for teaching GP residents. He did so on condition that he could be based at WGH Ilesha, and this was accepted. Soon after, the university appointed him a lecturer in General Practice in the Department of Community Health. He now heads a unit of Family Practice and Social Medicine within that Department, and contributes to undergraduate GP training. For me it is a dream come true. The wheel has turned full circle. When I left WGH in 1975 it was with a sense of unfinished business. The need for some kind of hospital-based general practice training was apparent. At Igbo-ora I had the opportunity to help develop the FMCGP programme, and now WGH Ilesha is proving a major centre for its promotion. The vision is back where it started.

WGH Ilesha receives a better deal

The name of the university was changed to Obafemi Awolowo University as a memorial to Chief Awolowo after his death in 1987. He had contributed so much to the Western Region and was the first Chancellor of the University. WGH Ilesha was now just one of the two hospitals remaining in the Obafemi Awolowo University Teaching Hospital Complex (OAUTHC). The Ife State Hospital was the other, and through many additions, had become the larger. In 1989 the Professor of Psychiatry at Ife, Dr Roger O. Makanjuola, was made the Chief Medical Director. He had developed a Psychiatric Ward and Day Care Centre at WGH Ilesha by modifying the facilities in the old maternity ward. He was the nephew of the King of Imesi-Ile, Oba Richard Makanjuola, the Owa-Ooye, and knew much about the background of the child health care at Imesi, and the long history of work at WGH Ilesha before it was taken over. More than any CMD before him he began to do his best to give Ilesha its fair share of resources. A weekly meeting with key members of staff gave them a share in decision making. An Ilesha/OAUTHC Liaison Committee with the obas of Ilesha and Imesi-Ile as members, the Lay President of the Methodist Church Nigeria (Ilesha Diocese) and other community representatives, was also started.

One problem in particular which Professor Makanjuola vowed to resolve was the chronic lack of water in the hospital. Supplies had become desperately short, and a bare minimum only was being maintained through trucking in water by 3000 gallon tanker, to be pumped into the many galvanized surface tanks which proliferated around every hospital building. Mr Lawrence Omole, businessman in town, did his best to secure a better water supply for the hospital through bore-holes. After several dry taps he told his driller to try once more, but that he would only be paid if he struck water. This time he was successful through a borehole near the stream. He received his fee, but perhaps the hole was not all that deep, and it did not last for long. It had been known from my time that the geology of the area was against finding borehole water because it was a solid ancient rock which lacked fissures where water could collect. Professor Makanjuola undertook to try an alternative solution which I had suggested through the construction of a dam across the Ayawo stream on the southern perimeter of hospital land. A feasibility survey showed that the flow should be sufficient. Professor Olikoye Ransome-Kuti, who was then Federal Minister of Health, took a great interest in the project and allocated funds. These was supplemented by money raised at a university Endowment Fund appeal in 1992, of which a part was for Ilesha water. The job has now been done. For the first time for many years the hospital has water in the taps.

The Wesley Guild heritage not forgotten

Links with overseas friends are always welcomed, and in particular with the Wesley Guilds. In November 1987 the Wesley Guilds in Britain recalled that the 75th Anniversary of the arrival of Dr J R C Stephens in Ilesha, January 12th 1913, was due shortly (1913-1988). A gift of books for the Library of the Nursing School and the General Practice residents was sent. Celebrations headed by the Nurses League were held in the following July. The nurses' Wesley Guild badges continue to be highly valued, and supplies are being maintained for all nurses still qualifying.

Recognition of the work done at Ilesha over the years has been given at the highest level, beginning with the MBE awarded to Dr Joyce Ludlow in June 1952, Miss Elsie Ludlow in May 1956, and to Miss Margaret Woodland in 1968, and received from the Queen in July 1969. I was given an OBE in 1974 'for services to Medicine in Nigeria', and received it from the hands of the Queen after leaving Ilesha in July 1975. Prof David Morley was given the King Faisal Award of £40,000 in 1982 for his book on *Paediatric Priorities in the Developing World* and the associated promotion of mother and child health world-wide, and was given the CBE in the New Year Honours List.

The traditional Nigerian way of giving honour came to my wife and me in the award of chieftaincies, first in Igbo-Ora in April 1983 (Aare Basegun and Ekerin Iyalaje - 'Medical Adviser' and 'Fourth Woman Activist', and then in Ilesha in May 1985 when the Owa-Obokun, Oba Adekunle Aromolaran II, conferred on us the titles of Oluawo and Yeye-Oluawo of Ilesha - 'Chief Medicine Man and his Helper'. Oluawo was the same title as that given to Dr Edward Hunter in 1936. Finally, chieftaincies were awarded in November 1987 by the Owa-Oye of Imesi-Ile to Professor David Morley, Miss Margaret Woodland (though unable to be present personally) and to Mrs Pearson and myself, in recognition of the vitally important work for child health done at Imesi-Ile and Ilesha in years past. They were the first Imesi-Ile chieftaincies to be given following Chief Makanjuola's crowning two years before.

Fig 10.1 *Chief Dr David Morley at Imesi-Ile, 1987 with Miss Remi Domingo, nursing sister*

CHAPTER 11

IS THAT IT?

The story has been told. Sad notes near the end may leave present day members of the Wesley Guild in Britain, and the many from around the world who worked there, wondering if their involvement with WGH Ilesha through all the years from 1912 to 1975 was only of passing moment, exciting while it lasted. Or can they feel that what was achieved has real significance for today?

I believe there is no doubt as to the lasting value. There are at least three areas in which the claim can be made - the revolution in child care, the training programmes pioneered which still continue, and the promotion of a balanced view of healing carried forward in the witness of the church today.

The revolution in child care

Methods which have spread from Ilesha around the world
WGH Ilesha has been the source of a new style of community child health care which has spread to all developing countries. The research which David Morley undertook in Ilesha and Imesi-Ile, 1956 to 1961, was to lay the foundation for a 'child health revolution'. The Under Fives Clinics at Imesi-Ile and WGH Ilesha set the pattern for the regular monitoring of children's health over the first five years by monthly weighing, and entering the weights on the graph of a growth chart. 'Morley weight-charts' are now printed in every conceivable language. Go to any developing country in the world and you will find them. Visitors to WGH Ilesha today can still see the 'Under Fives Welfare Clinic' building, the first such in the world. Acceptance of the methods pioneered have, in fact, been more rapid in other countries like Zambia and Papua New Guinea than in the rest of Nigeria. It is probable that few in WGH Ilesha, and the OAU teaching hospital as a whole, realise

the significance of what began on their own doorstep. The Federal Ministry of Health has incorporated this style of child health care into its Primary Care *Standing Orders* for Community Health Extension Workers, but all too few of the Local Government health centre staff put it in to practice. The vision still lies mainly with the church-related hospitals and health care services.

Christian Health Association of Nigeria (CHAN)
The inauguration of CHAN owed much to ideas generated at WGH Ilesha, and to its staff who gave of their time in its support. I was the first Chairman of CHAN's Primary Care Committee, but in 1984 it became possible to make this into a Primary Care Division (CHAN-PHC), and to appoint the Rev. Moses Thliza as the full-time leader. In February 1994 the first ten years of CHAN-PHC was celebrated in a major five-day conference at Jos in the central Plateau State of Nigeria. 200 were expected as participants, but 300 turned up, and somehow extra beds were found and food provided. Doctors, nurses, administrators and community health care personnel converged from all over the country. I was kindly invited, together with my wife, to give a key-note address. To look around that gathering, and to realise the tremendous work being done by church-related health workers, Methodist, Anglican, Catholic, Baptist, Brethren and many others, was heart-warming. None of them now receive any help from the government, yet they struggle on. In many aspects of their child care work they follow where WGH Ilesha first pioneered.

Training which continues

WGH Ilesha has been and still is an important centre for training. The commitment to the next generation is unbroken.

Nursing School
The long history of nursing and midwifery training within a Christian institution from the days of Stella Liony onwards, has given to Nigeria a cadre of dedicated women who have maintained the highest standards of their profession. In recent years men have been included too. Positive discrimination is no longer required. Nursing is not just knowledge and skills, but above all of attitudes, and the Christian spirit of service given

in love provides the surest motivation for good practice. The Guild badge, and the motto, 'One Heart One Way' has been respected and valued. It still is. Under the present secular management, those with a personal faith have continued down the years since take-over to set a high example to others, and one hopes and prays that God will continue to call the present generation of leaders to a similar commitment. They have a heritage to honour. The Nurses' League regularly meets on the first Saturday of July each year, and they start their gathering by singing their version of the Guild hymn (1) which ends with the verse:

> 'One heart, one way, take up the joyful song,
> Bring hope to those who still for healing long,
> We give ourselves in service now this day;
> Because we find in Christ, one heart, one way.'

Medical students and General Practice registrars
From the 1960s students from Ibadan found inspiration at Ilesha. Now, WGH as part of the Obafemi Awolowo University Teaching Hospital Complex, has a vital role in another medical school training the next generation of doctors for the country. The Methodist Church Nigeria, though not receiving WGH back into its proprietorship, can nevertheless be thankful that it is part of a respected university, and that its mission hospital origins and service through the years is not being wasted.

WGH Ilesha is also being given the opportunity to pioneer general practice training at undergraduate level, and to be a major support to the postgraduate training of General Practitioners throughout Nigeria. Dr E A Kuteyi FMCGP, has been appointed Faculty Board Secretary for the National Postgraduate Medical College, serving the whole country. He recently represented the Faculty at an international conference of the World Organization of General Practitioners (WONCA) in Hong Kong. There he found that the Nigerian General Practice training programme was the first in the world to prepare doctors for front-line medical care in district level rural hospitals. Other countries, like Nepal, India, and Malaysia are following a similar path. When I left WGH in 1975 to work with College of Medicine, Ibadan, it was to pass on the general practice skills learned at Ilesha to another generation of Nigerian medical students and doctors. Dr Kuteyi, the first to benefit, is now at Ilesha carrying on the same work, and, incidentally, with the same faith and motivation.

A balanced view of healing

Above all, WGH Ilesha was a mission enterprise, and who knows how much was done to help build God's Kingdom - 'on earth, as it is in heaven'? An international gazetteer published thirty years ago, which listed the main towns in Nigeria, noted, in the brief description of Ilesha, that 'Eighty per cent of the population was Christian due in part to the presence of a mission hospital in the town'. The hospital certainly helped the church to overcome cultural fears caused by illness, enabling people to experience the reality of God's loving care. In a country where the spiritual, mental and physical are all so closely interwoven, the hospital spread a balanced view of healing, whereby not only prayer, but also the advances accruing from scientific research and modern medicine are seen as equally gifts from God for us to use. Certainly the Methodist Church Nigeria maintains that balance. This is seen in the confidence of the church today in taking up fresh challenges in health care. The economy in Nigeria is very weak, and assistance from the church in Britain has been requested. The Guilds have again heard the call, and have decided to raise funds as a special project to mark the 100 years since the Wesley Guilds first started, 1896-1996.

The Centenary Guild Health Project
This has three main items.

1. **Bethesda Hospital, Ikachi, in Benue State**. This is a 60-bed rural Methodist hospital serving the Igede people, run by Nigerian doctors and nurses, and with a Methodist minister, the Rev. Sunday Idoko, as the Administrator. It had been pioneered previously by Dutch missionaries but they have now moved on, leaving behind an excellent set of aluminium-frame hospital buildings, and some rather old-fashioned residences. The scheme is to allow for improved water supply, and the introduction of solar-powered pumps and lighting. Around the hospital is a network of primary care centres, providing what could become a model 'district health service' (DHS). The DHS concept is central to the health care reform strategies being promoted by the World Health Organization. Making the system work in practice has proved difficult in the Nigerian government situation. Success at Bethesda could be a useful beacon for others to follow.

2. **Welfare Service, Uzuakoli Leprosy Centre, Abia State.** Christians have led the world in the care and cure of patients with leprosy, following the example of Jesus 'who stretched out his hand' to them in healing. Uzuakoli, in particular, has had an illustrious part in the fight against this disease, led by such great leprologists as Dr Frank Davey, Dr Stanley Browne and Dr Lykle Hogerzeil, and it was the place where, through the work of Dr John Lowe, the drug Dapsone was first proved to be able to provide a cure when given in low dosage for many years. Dapsone so revolutionized leprosy care throughout the world that many of the big 'leprosy colonies' became redundant as patients were discharged free of all infectivity and allowed to return to their home community. Patients brought late for treatment were often made non-infective but still had serious disabilities because of injury to feet and hands that no longer had the sense of pain to protect them from cuts and burns. For these patients continued residence was unavoidable while reconstructive surgery, physiotherapy and occupational therapy were applied. These techniques have revolutionized the outlook, and been a land-mark in restoring to many their personal dignity and ability to live independently. The Leprosy Hospital is now part of the government service, and Dr Joseph Chukwu, who has already served nine years has recently been appointed Medical Superintendent. An opportunity for further study in Leeds was given in 1995, and he has now returned to continue his dedicated leadership.

   The Welfare Service at Uzuakoli is managed by the Methodist Church, and the Rev. Raphael Opoko, given special health management training, has spearheaded this work. A major contribution is being made to the rehabilitation of the patients, and to ex-patients unable to return home, and excluded from society. Manufacturing splints and wheel-chairs, designing and repairing special shoes for those with disabilities, making roof-tiles and constructing wooden toys and educational equipment are among the skills taught. Items are sold where possible, but the service is only partially self-supporting. The **Motherless Babies' Home** which is run in association is serving another need where the outlook for such children is otherwise so bleak.

3. **The Amaudo Mental Health Care Centre, Itumbauzo, near Bende, Abia State.** Through the inspired leadership of Miss Ros Colwill this centre has pioneered the care and rehabilitation of mentally dam-

aged destitute persons, generally left to beg for survival, or death, at the roadside. Such people are approached and invited to come to Amaudo where they are washed, clothed, housed, fed and cared for in a loving community without walls. Up to eighty 'residents' live and eat together with 'helpers' (the staff), receiving simple medication as required. The big circle of bungalows are allocated to residents and helpers alternately, and at the centre of the circle is a Chapel of Peace where prayers are held morning and evening. Essentially it is the loving and accepting attitude of all which produces remission of psychiatric symptoms and gradual restoration of a sufficiently normal stable personality to allow residents to return to the communities which first turned them out. Scores of them have now been happily discharged, and collected with joy by their families. Some who reach only limited improvement are being housed in a second centre at Ntalakwu down the road, where slower progress is allowed for. Even there some have made themselves self-supporting through farming, trading, and the crafts they have learned.

Such has been the success rate of this venture that Amaudo has been made the corner-stone of a Community Psychiatric Service for the whole of Abia State, staffed by trained psychiatric nurses who at last find themselves effectively employed. Ros is now engaged in accepting residents formerly housed in the State's prison, primarily because of their mental problems but without any mental health care. Nigeria has never before seen such a humane and effective solution to the problem of mental destitutes. Indeed it may be a world first, destined to help mental patients in all developing countries. Small wonder that Ros, too, has been made a chief. The Methodist Church Nigeria has a precious work in its charge, and is thankful for international help to keep it going. I believe the Guild Centenary Project support might even lead to a more permanent commitment.

It all began in 1912. Through the years the giving and the praying and the costly service in front-line care has continued. Now the challenge to assist the church's healing ministry in Africa has been heard again. I have no doubt of the Guild response. Their faith is expressed in the Guild Centenary Hymn (2):

'Through the years of change and progress,
Shifts in thought and attitude;
We have found among God's people
Faith and hope and love renewed,
In the call to costly service
In the church and in the world.'

REFERENCES

Chapter 5

1. Morley DC. Medical service for children under five years of age in West Africa. *Trans Roy Soc Trop Med Hyg*, 1963; 57: 79-94.

2. King M.(ed). *Medical Care in Developing Countries*, 1966, OUP, Oxford.

3. Morley DC. *Paediatric Priorities in the Developing World*, 1973, Butterworths, London.

4. Pearson CA. *Medical Administration for Front-line Doctors*, 1990 (2nd edition 1995), FSG Communications, Cambridge.

5. Cannon DSH, Hartfield VJ. Obstetrics in a developing country. *J Obs Gyn Brit Cwlth*, 1964; 71: 940-950.

6. Editorial. Obstetrics in developing countries. *Lancet*, 1965 (i): 791.

7. Food and Agriculture Organization. *Reports to the Government of Nigeria on Home Gardens for Improved Nutrition*, 1969, 1971 and 1973, FFHC/FAO; 39, 75 and 90, FAO Rome.

8. Cunningham N. The under fives clinic - what difference does it make? *J Trop Ped Env Child Health*, 1978; 24: 239-334.

Chapter 6

1. Wright HJ, Morley DC. 'Encephalitis tremens'. *Lancet*, 1958; 1: 871-873.

2. Pearson CA, Moore DL, David-West TS. Virus studies in Ilesha Shakes. *W Afr Med J*, 1973; 22: 20-22.

3. Cannon DSHC. Malaria and prematurity in the Western Region of Nigeria. *Brit Med J*, 1958; 2: 453-456.

4. Morley DC. Childhood tuberculosis in rural areas of West Africa. *W Afr Med J*, 1959; 8: 225.

5. Knox G, Morley DC. Twinning in Yoruba women. *J Obs Gyn Brit Comm*, 1960; 67: 981-984.

6. Morley DC. Measles in Nigeria. *Am J Dis Child*, 1962; 103: 220-223.

7. Cox ML. Symphysiotomy in Nigeria. *J Obs Gyn Brit Cwlth*, 1966; 73: 237.

8. Mulligan TO. Typhoid fever in young children. *Brit Med J*, 1971; 4: 665-667.

9. Hartfield VJ. The role of paramedical personnel in family planning programmes. *W Afr Med J*, 1968; 17: 225-226.

10. Pearson CA. Hypochromia as a clinical sign of tuberculosis in the tropics. *Tubercle*, 1978; 59: 111-119.

11. Pearson CA. Hypomelanosis as an aid to early recognition of tuberculosis in the African. *Trop Doctor*, 1989; 19: 188.

12. Pearson CA. Hypomelanosis in tuberculosis - unrelated to anaemia. *E Afr Med J*, 1990; 67: 419-426.

13. Pearson CA. Thiacetazone toxicity in the treatment of tuberculosis patients in Nigeria. *J Trop Med Hyg*, 1978; 81: 238-242.

14. Pearson CA. Early protected weight bearing in African patients with fracture of the femur. *Injury*, 1977; 9: 89-92.

Chapter 11

1. Wilson KD. Wesley Guild Hymn (verse 4, adapted), in Ilesha WGH 1974-1975 Hospital Report.

2. Carveley K. Centenary Guild Hymn (verse 2, part), 1995.

INDEX OF NAMES

People, Places, Organizations and Qualifications